A

𝕭rief 𝔐emoir

OF THE

REV. SAMUEL B. ARDAGH,

A.M., T.C.D.,

LATE RECTOR OF BARRIE AND INCUMBENT OF SHANTY BAY,
LAKE SIMCOE, UPPER CANADA.

EDITED BY THE
REV. SAMUEL J. BODDY, M.A.

For Private Circulation only.

TORONTO:
PRINTED BY ROWSELL AND HUTCHISON.
1874.

MEMOIR

OF THE

REV. S. B. ARDAGH.

SOME men there are so connected with the great events of the generation to which they belong, that their lives may be considered historical. Whether good or bad, they stand forth so conspicuously, that it is impossible to overlook them.

Others again, and this is true of the great mass, live and die in obscurity: their names being unknown beyond the little circle of which they have been the blessing or the curse. A few years or months after their consignment to the earth, and the memory of them has passed away.

There is yet another class which lies midway between these two, a class neither widely famous, nor yet entirely unknown. These last were in their day honoured and blessed above many; but not sufficiently so to excite any large amount of public attention. They were not exactly heroes, and fame therefore has little to say of them. Still their names are treasured in the hearts of many a sorrowing survivor, and affection, if nothing more, forbids that the grave should close over their remains without some effort to rescue them from oblivion. Hence the publication of not a few memoirs, which, in themselves, possess little to attract the notice of the general reader. Such memoirs are written, not in the vain hope of awakening permanent or universal interest—not because they contain any thing which the world cannot afford to lose—but simply because they are demanded by the voice of friendship. If so much goodness were allowed to pass away unchronicled, many would be grievously disappointed who desired to possess some record of it, more desirable and accurate than can be supplied by their own memories.

It is to a memoir of this kind that the reader's attention is asked in the following pages.

Many clergymen have occupied higher positions in the Church than he to whom these pages are devoted: many have deservedly won for themselves a greater reputation for learning and ability. But few, perhaps, have been more useful or respected; and scarcely any more generally beloved. Even outside the sphere to which his labours were limited for the greater part of his ministerial career, he was well-known as a valiant champion of the Truth; but within it, by those who profited by his labours, and especially within his own family circle, he was loved and revered as comparatively few men are when living; and mourned for, as men seldom are, on his departure. It is to these loving and mourning friends that the following brief sketch of his life and character is offered.

The Rev. SAMUEL BROWN ARDAGH, was born in Fethard, in the County of Tipperary, Ireland, on the 8th of April, 1803 He was the eldest son of the Rev. Arthur Ardagh, A.M., for some time fellow of Trinity College, Dublin, and subsequently Rector of Moyglare, County of Meath. His mother was Anne, daughter of Samuel Brown, of Fethard, a gentleman of independent means.

In a work by the recently deceased Master of the Rolls, the Right Hon. John Edward Walsh, entitled "Ireland, Sixty Years ago," Arthur Ardagh is spoken of as a man of profound scholarship, and of wild and restless temper Being the intimate friend of the unfortunate Robert Emmett, and of others who were mixed up in the political troubles of the latter part of the last century, he became for a time an object of suspicion to the Government. At their instance he was expelled by the College authorities, but some years later was reinstated in his fellowship, with ample acquittal from the charge of rebellion.

We learn by some early records that the family of Ardagh, or Ardaff (the name is so termed indifferently in the Herald's books), were settled and possessed of lands near Tullamore, in the Kings County, in the reign of Edward I. The traditions of the family point to a Welsh origin, and they are supposed to have made their exodus from Wales in the earlier part of that reign. Later on they appear on the page of local history as doing homage for lands held from the English Crown, and in the time of the Tudors as holding positions of civil trust. The extensive estates possessed by the family at an early period, melted away under the successive extravagance of several generations. The last lands possessed by them, passed, in the time of Mr. Ardagh's great-grandfather, into the hands of the Earl of Charleville. The large family of brothers and sisters, consisting of fourteen children, of whom the subject of this memoir was the eldest, were born to no inheritance but what they could win for themselves.

Two members of his family, a brother and sister, followed him to Canada. The former,

John Russell, practised as a medical man, for many years, in the town of Barrie, where he was universally esteemed, and died in 1868. The latter, Ellen Power, married Thomas, the eldest son of the late respected James Dallas, Esquire, of Orillia, and has rested for many years in the cemetery there.

No papers remain to shew in what year Mr. Ardagh entered Trinity College; but at the age of nineteen he resolved to relieve his father from the cost of his support and education. From this time, till he entered the Church, he supported himself by tuition; having, before he became Tutor of his College, been engaged in that capacity in a private family. He graduated in February, 1827, and in the month of June, the same year, was admitted to the Diaconate by the Bishop of Meath. Immediately afterwards he was appointed Curate assistant to his father, and a year later was ordained Priest by the same Prelate. With regard to his character at this time, it was in many respects most attractive. While passing through College he was one of the gayest and brightest members of a society which even then retained the prestige of the earlier brilliance which characterized it before the union of the Kingdoms. Gifted with a handsome person, and with graceful and genial manners, a geniality which survived even to his latest days, with more than ordinary conversational talent, a clever *raconteur*, accomplished in manly exercises, particularly distinguished for his daring horsemanship, a man to whom physical fear or moral cowardice was unknown, enthusiastic in conception, and impetuous in action, we can well believe the statements of his contemporaries that he was a favorite in society. There is, however, reason to fear that although realising to a certain extent the responsibility of the solemn office which he was about to enter, he was still very far from that earnest desire to win souls for Christ, which should be the highest aspiration of a Christian minister.

It pleased God, however, to give him the inestimable advantage of an earnest and Christian woman for a wife, one whose graces of intellect and character were recognized by all with whom she came in contact, and in whose loving and gentle companionship his character, as years went on, underwent a decided change for the better. Of her whose influence extended over his whole life, it is fitting that a few words should be spoken here.

Shortly after he was ordained Priest, he married Martha, the youngest daughter of the late Richard Anderson, Esquire, County Cavan, formerly an officer in the 22nd Regiment of Light Dragoons, who had retired on half-pay, on his early marriage. Mr. Anderson was a man of honorable character and unsullied integrity, of a most amiable disposition, and above all a true Christian. Although an invalid for the last fifteen years of his life, his influence on his daughter's character was deep and lasting, though perhaps she was mainly indebted for an admirable training to her mother, a woman of singular ability and masculine force of character; as well as to her uncle, Col. John Anderson, of the 4th Light Dragoon Guards, A. D. C. to H. R. H. the Duke of York, then Commander-in-Chief. Col. Anderson combined the qualities of a brave and distinguished soldier with a Christian excellence and stainless repute—in those days but rarely to be met with in military circles. Being himself childless he was able to devote much attention, during the leisure of his later life, to the education of his brother's children. For some years this uncle resided in the same neighbourhood, and later on the deep anxiety he felt for these children is amply evinced in the numerous letters of precept and guidance, still extant, which they received from him. Nor was the influence of his bright example and earnest admonitions exerted in vain. To this, in a great degree, his niece, Mrs. Ardagh, was undoubtedly indebted for the excellent principles she uniformly displayed through life.

Mr. Ardagh's first acquaintance with his future wife, was at Killesandra, where he was spending a summer vacation with his college friend, her cousin, afterwards the Rev. Arthur Moneypeny. Three years later they were married, in October, 1828, in Dublin, and immediately proceeded to Waterford, where he had been appointed to the Curacy of St. Patrick's, in that city.

The ancient city of Waterford, made memorable in old time by the fierce conflicts of the aboriginal Irish with the Danes, who have left, as a memorial of their supremacy, a Round Tower on the Quay, built by Reginald the Dane, and called by his name, and later still, the scene of Strongbow's landing, and marriage to Eva, daughter of the King of Leinster, and the temporary residence of two English sovereigns—was for fourteen years the home of Mr. Ardagh, and the birthplace of his children.

The early days of his ministry were days when party spirit ran high in the South of Ireland; and very often at this period Mr. Ardagh risked his life by his outspoken attachment to Protestant truths. One of the objects he had most at heart was the conversion of the Roman Catholics, and he was greatly interested in the Irish Home Mission. The main object of this Society was the introduction of the Irish language, by the Clergy, in their preaching and ministry amongst the peasantry. This scheme would seem to have been one which, if carried out with patient energy, would have done as much to evangelize and redeem the Church in Ireland, as church rates and wealthy endowments have done to smother it. While engaged in this work Mr Ardagh travelled through the Counties of Limerick and Kerry, and gained experience which in another country was of great use to him. He always bitterly lamented that this Missionary work was given up.

While zealous for the conversion of his Roman Catholic fellow countrymen, and fearless in denouncing the errors of their religion, he was always to them personally a kind friend, ever desirous of ministering to their temporal as well as spiritual wants.

He was the chief promoter and active worker in an association for the relief of the destitute, the majority of those aided being Roman Catholics. On several recent occasions members of his family visiting the neighbourhood of his old home, heard with joy, after so many years, his name still spoken of by persons of that faith, with affection and respect, they even recalling with gratitude special acts of kindness done them.

Many will remember 1832 as the year of the cholera. This terrible disease raged with special vehemence in Ireland, and Mr. Ardagh was often called upon to minister to the bodily no less than the spiritual necessities of those who were stricken by it. The cholera hospitals were crowded, and from them the dead were carried by hundreds. Nurses fled in dismay, but Mr. Ardagh, not confining himself to their spiritual needs, performed every office, even the most repulsive, for the dying and the dead, and scarcely left his post night or day. Among the many ministers who distinguished themselves at this time of trial, he was one of the most devoted.

Though his life, during his long residence in Waterford, was comparatively uneventful, we may hope that his many plans for the spiritual good of his people were not unblessed. In connection with these we must speak of the Rev. Richard Ryland, his life-long friend, who, like the subject of this memoir, though occupying no honoured or prominent place in the world's esteem, yet amongst the many faithful clergymen then in Waterford, was one of the most self-denying servants of Christ.

The Sunday School was to them an object of great and prayerful interest. It was characterized by this peculiar feature: children belonging to the different Established Churches of the city met under one roof, subject to the superintendence of all the clergy. The number who attended it (at this time upwards of 700) was remarkably large in proportion to the small Protestant population, and its efficiency was great, as none but Christian men and women were selected for the office of teachers. To secure this end, weekly teachers' meetings were held for the earnest study of the Holy Scriptures, with fervent prayer for a blessing on their work.

An interesting feature of Christian society in Waterford was the Monday evening meetings, held in the New Room, Mall. The first Monday evening in the month was devoted to the discussion of Missionary work all over the world; the second, to the spiritual advancement of soldiers and sailors; the third, to Sunday School progress; the fourth, to the furtherance of Evangelical truth on the continent of Europe; and the fifth, to the promotion of Christianity among the Jews. All these subjects were considered in a spirit of fervent prayer, and strangers from a distance were often invited to speak on these and kindred matters, and were always listened to by crowded and interested audiences. A volume of hymns was selected and published for the use of these assemblies.

At the close of the year 1832, Mr. Ardagh went to Dublin and took his degree of A. M., with which honor he was content, declining to accept the nominally higher title of D. C. L., which was afterwards more than once tendered to him by a Canadian University.

Among the causes which led Mr. Ardagh to entertain the idea of leaving his native country, the principal was his exposure to various outrages, as the following incidents will tend to illustrate.

He had been the means of converting a young woman in humble life from the errors of Romanism. She was suffering from a lingering disease, and as the time of her death approached, the persecutions of her relatives induced him to comply with her request, to remove her to a place where she could die in peace. Late that night, while dining with some friends, intelligence reached him that she had been removed with violence. After some search he found her in a wretched room at the top of a four-storey house, in the worst part of the town. The room was crowded with women; and some priests were endeavouring to induce her to recant. He was with difficulty allowed to approach the bed, when she implored him not to leave her. He was thereupon hustled to the window by the women, and half thrust out. He appealed to the priests present to save him from being murdered, and, owing to their interference, was allowed to descend the stairs, being several times struck from behind, and narrowly escaping with his life. He remained on the watch for some time, and found her towards morning left perfectly alone. Summoning the assistance of some friends, he removed her to her former place of shelter, where she died calmly, in a few hours, in the faith of Christ. Whilst officiating at her funeral, Mr. Ardagh was assailed with stones and missiles, and was finally himself thrust into the grave, which the crowd hastily commenced to fill up. He was again Providentially rescued, and only escaped by running off at his utmost speed, and leaping over the churchyard-wall.

At this time Mr. Ardagh lived at Kingville, more than a mile from the city, and was constantly in the habit of returning home at a late hour. Threats were not wanting that the loneliness of the road would be taken advantage of by his enemies to do him bodily injury; and in proof that this was not mere idle talk, a gentleman was found one morning, on the direct road to Mr. Ardagh's house, nearly beaten to death: the circumstances clearly pointing to an attempt on the life of the fearless clergyman.

At those times, in Waterford, elections were always the occasion of riotous outbreaks—religious and political differences being inextricably blended.

During one of these stormy periods, Mr. Ardagh happened to be returning to town from some distance in the country. He was driving in a gig, accompanied by his cousin, the late Dr. John Ardagh, of Orillia. His route was along the Quay, where the infuriated mob with a wild yell rushed upon him, and having taken down the chain which guarded it, backed his horse towards the river. The wheels were already slipping over the edge of the stone work, when the powerful horse which he drove, maddened by the shouts and pressure of the crowd, reared and plunged violently forward, scattering his assailants. Thus, by the Providence of God, he was once again saved from death. In the spring of 1842 he received a final warning. His mother-in-law found, one morning, near the house, a child's head, lately exhumed, to which was attached a notice threatening him with a similar fate, if he did not desist from speaking against the Roman Catholic religion.

The anxiety consequent upon this state of affairs so preyed upon the delicate health of his wife, that he decided upon the important step of leaving his native country. The call, at this time, of the Society for the Propagation of the Gospel for Missionary labour in Canada, turned his attention in that direction, and through the medium of this Society he entered into correspondence with Col. O'Brien, of "The Woods," County of Simcoe, with reference to the extensive missionary field, of which Shanty Bay was the head-quarters. As the result of this communication, Mr. Ardagh, in faith, and after much prayer, decided on entering upon this large and unknown sphere of labour.

Before he set sail he was waited on by a deputation, headed by the Mayor of Waterford, who, in the name of the Protestant congregation of the Union of St. Patrick, and other friends, lay and clerical, residing in Waterford and its vicinity, presented him with the following very kind and laudatory address, together with a substantial mark of their esteem, in the shape of a purse, containing the sum of £130 sterling, and a very fine copy of the Holy Scriptures :—

"REV. AND DEAR SIR,—We, the Protestant Congregation of the Union of St. Patrick, together with your fellow labourers in Christ's vineyard, and others connected with you by the ties of friendship and esteem, resident in this city and its vicinity, having heard of your intended removal to Canada, unite in expressing to you our sense of the loss which we, in common with the Church in this City and neighborhood, must sustain by your proposed departure from the scene of your past labors.

"We cannot permit your ministry among us to close without recording the high opinion which we unanimously entertain of the manner in which, during a period of fourteen years, you have discharged the duties of your arduous calling : for, whether we regard you as the bold and uncompromising preacher of the gospel, or exhibiting in private life the meekness and humility of the Christian pastor, as the kind, and assiduous instructor of infancy in the early lessons of truth and holiness, or ministering spiritual consolation beside the couch of suffering humanity, your conduct has uniformly given evidence of ardent and entire devotion to the cause of Him under whose banner you have enlisted.

"But, however deep and heartfelt our regret at your departure, we have at least the consolation of reflecting that your removal will introduce you into a new and wider sphere of Christian duty, and afford you further opportunity and more extended means of usefulness ;

and we humbly pray that wherever your services shall hereafter be employed, you may, through Divine grace, be enabled so to feed the flock committed to your charge, that when the Chief Shepherd shall appear, you may obtain a crown of glory that fadeth not away.

"We entreat your acceptance of the gift which accompanies this declaration of our feelings, in further testimony of the sentiments to which we have endeavoured to give expression: And assuring you with great sincerity that we shall never cease to take a lively interest in all that concerns your future happiness and welfare.

"Believe us to remain,
Reverend and Dear Sir,
Your faithful and attached Friends."

Nor was this the only testimonial which Mr. Ardagh received at this time. Another flattering address, engrossed on parchment, and under the Episcopal seal of the Diocese, was presented to him in the name of the Dean and Chapter, and Clergy, of the Diocese of Waterford, who, in the summer of 1842, were assembled in the Cathedral Church, on the occasion of the Bishop's visitation. From the language of that address, which we give below, it will be seen that Mr. Ardagh had won for himself a high place in the opinion of his brother clergymen, many of whom must have had ample opportunity of knowing his character; and this testimony to his worth, is the more valuable because it is comparatively seldom that anything of the kind is given to a clergyman on his leaving one Diocese for another.

"WE, the Dean and Chapter, and Clergy, of the Diocese of Waterford, assembled at the Bishop's visitation, held in the Cathedral Church, on Tuesday, 5th July, 1842, cannot let pass this last occasion of meeting you officially without an expression of our affectionate esteem for you as a brother, minister, and friend, and of our sincere and conscientious regret that you are about to leave our Diocese. It is not for us to offer an opinion upon your conduct, during the period of fifteen years that you have been a curate amongst us. It would be unsuitable for us to assume the chair of judgment—and happily the unanimous testimony of those among whom you ministered renders it unnecessary; but we may be permitted to tender you our warmest wishes for your health and prosperity, both spiritual and temporal, and our unaffected assurance that, in your departure, we lose the sympathy, counsel, and co-operation of a kind and affectionate friend. Accept our heartfelt prayers, and remember us in a distant land as brothers "with whom you took sweet counsel, and walked to the House of God in company."

In the month of August, 1842, he sailed, with his family, from the port of Waterford, in the brig "Thistle," a timber ship trading between that port and Quebec (those were not the days of ocean steamers), and forty-six days elapsed before they reached their destination. Though a long voyage, it was full of sunshine and calm, and a time of both mental and physical rest, after the wearing anxiety of the past few years.

The first time they touched the shores of the new country was at the Quarantine Station of Grosse Isle. Those green fields and pretty white French houses, were a refreshing rest to the eye, which had so long wandered over a waste of waters. Mr. Ardagh and his wife, true lovers of scenery, appreciated to the full the magnificence of the broad St. Lawrence; and the thousands who have looked upon Quebec for the first time, can understand the effect produced upon the voyagers, as rounding the Isle of Orleans, the city, in the picturesque beauty of its commanding position, with its ancient citadel, glittering spires and roofs, reflected back the brilliance of the autumn sunshine. At Quebec they were welcomed by Mrs. Ardagh's brother, the Rev. Richard Anderson, who had been for some time missionary in a remote parish in that Diocese, and whose clerical friends there tendered to Mr. Ardagh and his family kind hospitality during their short stay.

In those primitive times the journey from Quebec to Toronto occupied a fortnight, as the only water route to the Upper Province was by the Rideau Canal, passing through Bytown, then a green and secluded village, now Ottawa, the capital of the Dominion.

On leaving Toronto, Mr. Ardagh's family proceeded on their journey in a more simple fashion. There being but one small stage-coach, the greater number of the party were conveyed up Yonge Street on baggage waggons, to Holland Landing, and thence across Lake Simcoe in the Steamer "Simcoe," to Shanty Bay, where they arrived on the 7th October, 1842. Here the party were received and hospitably entertained for some time by Col. and Mrs. O'Brien. During this pleasant visit was laid the foundation of that warm and abiding friendship between the families, which has lasted through so many years of change and trial.

The extraordinary loveliness of the autumn of 1842, has been chronicled by the pen of Nathaniel Hawthorne. Never had the vivid colouring of the woods, the slumberous atmosphere, and the unruffled waters peculiar to the Indian summer, been more beautiful than on the October day when Mr. Ardagh first saw the spot which was to be his home for so many years

The parsonage house, which had been occupied by his predecessor, Mr. Bartlett, consisting as it did of only three small rooms, was quite inadequate to the requirements of Mr. Ardagh's family, consisting of his wife, his mother-in-law, seven children, governess, and servants: one other member, Miss Anderson, having remained in Quebec, with her brother. Under these circumstances, Mr. John Whitley, a single gentleman in the neighborhood, kindly placed his house at their disposal, and into it, as winter approached, they removed, and there remained till the following June, when the parsonage house, to which Mr. Ardagh had made a substantial addition at his own expense, was ready for their reception.

We subjoin a reminiscence from the pen of a member of the party who accompanied Mr. Ardagh to Canada:—

"How vividly upon my memory are photographed the recollections of those days of travel. The sluggish Holland River, whose pale marsh grasses undulated with the movement of the paddle-wheels; the broad bright lake, the noble estuary of Kempenfeldt Bay, whose far-stretching shores, broken in outline by bay and headland, were vestured and crowned with the glory of the autumn woods. Four miles from the entrance, on the north shore, we steamed up to the wharf at Shanty Bay, a rude wooden pier, the foreground of a sylvan recess surrounded by wooded heights. The face of these low cliffs was clothed with the luxuriant foliage of wild raspberry and vine, and through their tangled bloom rocky paths led to the road above, a road by courtesy only, it being a chaos of mud holes, dry in hot weather, and bridged over by 'corduroys' in hopelessly miry places. Here we always found the earliest wild violets and hepaticas of spring, and its picturesque woodland scenery atoned for the marshy condition of the pathway. Two days later, in company with our kind host and hostess, and their children, we attended our first service in the church at Shanty Bay, embarking at the same rustic wharf, in order to avoid the worst half of the road to the church, then almost impassable from recent rains. The affluence of light and color which characterized that Indian summer, made a vivid impression on those fresh from a paler and less glowing atmosphere. Here we saw, in all their beauty, the brilliant clearness of the inland waters, the circling ring of green woods surrounding the 'clearing' where we landed, where, from the sombre hues of the ancient pine forests, and the brighter tints of later growth, gleamed out the crimson and gold, the russet and purple of a Canadian autumn. In the background of the clearing the little white church seemed to nestle in the bosom of the woods, whilst in the foreground the tiny rustic parsonage, surrounded by *debris*, fallen timber, and stumps of trees, indicative of a new clearing, and itself half veiled by low shrubbery, trailing Virginia creeper, and tall rank grasses, was not out of unison with the wildness of the surrounding landscape. Many will remember this sunny spot at a later time, when, in a still rustic, but more ample habitation, with long, low, vine-covered verandah, a host of friends were generally found and always welcome. The surroundings had then more the aspect of lawn and garden; and at the foot of the green-sloping land the water chimed and murmured through the summer days, or broke in louder resonance on autumn nights. The little point of silvery pebbles which stretched into the blue water to the right of The Parsonage, was called by the little ones 'Rosy' Point, because of the bloom of wild roses, which blended with the emerald foliage of early summer. Towards this, and along the shore, ran a shady, woodland walk, so close to the lake that in spring, when the waters were high, the waves often broke over the pathway."

Six miles from this quiet habitation, at the head of Kempenfeldt Bay, was situated the town of Barrie, in those early days a mere hamlet, although possessing the public buildings, which were essential to its position as chief town of the then District of Simcoe. At the Spring and Fall Assizes held here, the Judge was often accompanied by members of the Toronto bar: the local bar being, at that time, very limited in numbers. Occasionally, both bench and bar were entertained at The Parsonage after a fashion which combined many of the accessories of aboriginal simplicity with the amenities of cultivated society. This odd combination of surroundings was not unusual at those times.*

---

* On one occasion when Mr. Ardagh was journeying through the woods, searching out the far-scattered habitations of his parishioners, he came upon a small log house in a very lonely situation. As he entered, the mistress of the house rose to meet him, from scrubbing the floor. Her dress, and the furniture of the cabin, were of the humblest description; but on a rude side-board was piled an array of glittering silver plate, with a heraldic blazon which spoke of an ancient name and better days.

In the same month the late lamented Bishop Strachan paid his first visit to Shanty Bay, to hold a confirmation; and the gentlemen of the neighbourhood were invited to meet him at The Parsonage. The house was built of logs, and the unfinished condition of the interior may be inferred from the fact, that the walls of the room in which they dined were roughly hewn by the woodman's axe, the rafters being visible over head. This visit of the Bishop, though often repeated in after years, made a deep impression on the children, whose hearts were quite won by his kindly genial manner; and in the published account of his visitation tour that year, he makes a pleasant reference to his visit to Shanty Bay.

It may here be mentioned that in the course of years the original tenement fell to decay, and Mr. Ardagh, a second time, made a large outlay in providing a suitable dwelling for his family. On this occasion, with very little extraneous help, he managed to erect the present complete and comfortable residence, in which he spent the remainder of his days.

The mission in connection with Shanty Bay was very extensive, so much so that but little more than occasional services could possibly be held anywhere. It embraced an area of over

110 miles by 50 miles, and consisted of the townships of Oro, Medonte, Flos, Innisfil, Vespra, Mono, Essa, Euphrasia, Sunnidale, Nottawasaga, and St. Vincent. This field of labour extended over what is now divided into twelve parishes. Soon after his arrival he was appointed first Rector of Barrie, the county town, much more considerable than Shanty Bay, and distant from it six miles. To many persons it was matter of regret that he did not live in Barrie rather than at Shanty Bay. But in this latter place alone was there any provision for a clergyman. Through the exertions of Col. O'Brien and his English friends, a sum was raised sufficient for a small endowment of about £70 a year, and a substantial mud-brick church was built, in architectural appearance vastly superior to the barn-like edifices of the period. The church at Barrie was a frame building, erected by Admiral Robert O'Brien, through whose influence it was endowed as a Rectory, by his friend Sir John Colborne, afterwards Lord Seaton. The Clergy Reserve lands which formed the endowment, were, at the time, of nominal value, and being unoccupied, yielded little, if any return.

After Mr. Ardagh's appointment to Barrie, he began to realize the arduous character of the work assigned to a missionary in a new country. He had now to hold three full services every Sunday, travelling never less than twelve miles, in all kinds of weather; while during the week he held four services at distant stations. Periodically, his duties were of a still more laborious nature. The roads in the County of Simcoe, were at that time among the worst in Upper Canada, and were often only passable on horseback. He made at least two rounds during the year to the more distant settlements, proclaiming His Master's message. He was a man of great powers of endurance, and on one of these occasions, being in company with the resident Judge, who was on circuit, he travelled over 100 miles in the saddle, within eight days, having fourteen full services, and preaching or lecturing twenty times within that period. On many occasions in the course of his circuits, he administered the rites of the Church to many who had been without Christian ministrations for many years, often baptizing whole families.

Few but those who have had practical experience can realize the labour and the danger incident to a missionary life in Canada, or can appreciate the nature and extent of the hardship to be endured in the performance of such duties. The wretched accommodation, the scanty and far from nourishing diet, common among the earlier settlers,* coupled with great responsibility and fatigue, which weighed heavily on mind and body, injured Mr. Ardagh's constitution, and sowed the seeds of a subsequently mortal disease.

On one occasion he lost his way in the woods, during a heavy snow storm, and only succeeded, under Providence, in extricating himself from so desperate a position, by tying his horse to a tree, and then proceeding on foot, taking the precaution to mark all the trees he passed in a direct line. When, at length, he reached a shanty, he was almost fainting from exhaustion; and his horse, when discovered by means of the marked trees, was well nigh buried in snow. On another occasion he was precipitated, along with his horse, into a deep gravel pit, which had been left unmarked. Though severely shaken, he managed after some time to remount, having yet more than thirty miles to go. His horse accomplished this long distance without much apparent effort, but dropped dead when

---

* As a beverage, tea being almost unattainable, the early settlers used an infusion of the leaves of the hemlock tree; having, as the staple article of food, salt pork and cakes made of flour and water, known by the name of "dampers."

the journey was over, having sustained some internal injury. On another occasion he had to ride for his life through burning forests, and not seldom was he compelled to swim his horse through swollen streams

Those who have lived in the back townships of Canada, in the neighbourhood of the smaller lakes, will remember the extent to which persons travelled over their frozen surface, and especially when the spring rains and melting of the snow had rendered the mud roads almost impassable. This mode of travelling, though it had its advantages, was often very dangerous, and many lives were lost in consequence. One Sunday morning, having taken to the ice of Kempenfeldt Bay, in preference to the road, to attend service in Barrie, the treacherous surface gave way under him, he having left his cutter to ascertain whether a crack could be safely crossed by his horse. Fortunately, no worse results followed than the discomfort of frozen clothing, and the inconvenience of having to continue his journey in another way. On a similar occasion, when on horseback, his horse broke through the edge of one of the cracks, and precipitated them into the water, and for two hours Mr. Ardagh struggled to extricate himself. When nearly exhausted with exposure and fatigue, assistance arrived in answer to his calls, and relieved him from his difficulties.

Many such hair-breadth escapes might be mentioned. Mr. Ardagh's courage and nerve were unflinching. He was careless of danger, even to recklessness; and neither danger nor difficulties ever deterred him from the performance of his duty; and so cheerful and elastic was his disposition, that on his return home he would recount his adventures with smiles, never even seeming to recognize the hardships he had undergone.

The following extracts from his Diary bear the date of 1842, and will give some idea of his labours, from the time of his arrival in Canada:

"Oct. 7th—Arrived at Shanty Bay, where I am to be located. No house ready to receive my large family. Was hospitably taken into the house of Col. O'Brien.

· Oct. 9th—Commenced my ministry by holding Divine Service at Shanty Bay, at 11 o'clock, a.m., and 3 o'clock, at Barrie Church, six miles distant. Was occupied partly in visiting from house to house in Barrie and various parts of the neighbourhood, and partly in endeavouring to get persons to undertake to build an addition to The Parsonage.

Dec. 8th—To-day proceeded to Innisfil, and taking a neighbour (though it was a severe snow storm) who kindly volunteered to act as my guide into the backwoods, where I could not have found my way. Visited eleven families, who all received me with much apparent joy. I returned thirteen miles, after dark, in a snow storm. I am encouraged : the harvest is plenteous, but the labourers are few in this land.

Dec. 9th—Rode to-day sixteen miles through the bush,—the track being so full of mud-holes, it took me five hours to accomplish it,—to Mr. Ryall's, Oro, where I held Divine Service, and preached to about twenty-five persons. Slept there. Left, after breakfast, for Mrs. Hall's, four miles distant, where I had service, and preached to about forty. Proceeded home by Penetanguishene Road, a circuitous route of twenty-four miles, in order to determine on a central place to have meeting. Visited several persons on the way home, where I arrived about an hour after nightfall. Congregation at Barrie has increased from forty to upwards of a hundred.

Dec. 19th—Rode this morning to Henry's School House, at Essa, a distance of sixteen miles, where I held service at eleven o'clock. Congregation about fifty.

Dec. 21st—Rode five miles into the bush to

meet a small settlement of coloured people; the only poor I have yet met with. They promised to attend the church at Shanty Bay.

Dec. 22nd—Went to Barrie to visit.

Dec. 25th—Large congregation at Barrie to-day. About thirty at the Lord's Supper. Congregation at Shanty Bay, forty-six.

Dec. 26th—Rode to Barrie. Had an application, by letter, from friends of the Union Sabbath School, to preach a sermon in aid of their funds. My answer was, that before I could do so I should first see whether the friends of the school could so arrange that I should have the superintendence. Received another letter requesting me to meet the friends and teachers of the school, in order to come to an understanding.

Dec. 28th—Met the friends of the Union Sabbath School, of which a worthy man, an operative tanner, was President. After some discussion, in which I claimed control as Minister of Barrie, which they would not permit, I determined to organize one of my own.

Dec. 30th—Rode to Innisfil to-day. Visited eleven families.

Jan. 1st. 1843—Congregation at Barrie numbered one hundred and fifty : at Shanty Bay, fifty, and ten communicants.

Jan. 3rd—Divine Service at Innisfil, at the School House: thirty present. A heavy snow storm previous night kept some away.

Jan. 10th—Held service at the School House, twelve miles off, on the Penetanguishene Road. Present, about thirty. Went from there to Barrie to meet some persons who offered themselves as teachers in the Sunday School about to be opened. It was arranged that the school be opened on Sunday week, in the church, solely under my superintendence.

Jan. 12th—Divine Service on the Lake Shore, in an unoccupied house, about thirteen miles off. Fifty present. Baptized nine children.

Jan. 13th—Service at Mrs. Hall's. Congregation about forty. Baptized two children. Missed my way coming home, and lost eight miles.

Jan. 16th—Service at Essa. The congregation increasing, and very attentive. Number to-day, sixty. On to Mr. Osler's: from thence to Georgina, to attend the Quarterly Clerical Meeting. Arrived at the Rev. Mr. Gibson's late in the evening of 17th, together with Rev. Messrs. Meyerhoffer, Street, Townley, and McGeorge.

Jan. 18th—Held our meeting at 10 o'clock. Commenced with prayer Had the service for the Ordaining of Priests. Read 10th chapter of

Hebrews, and examined it verse by verse, till two o'clock. At three o'clock we went to the church, and held service.

Jan. 19th—Left next morning for Newmarket, where a public meeting was to be held to form a Church Society. I read prayers: Mr. Osler preached. Was much gratified by the large, attentive, and respectable congregation. This is a very useful addition and improvement of our clerical meetings in the old country, as it interests the laity in our proceedings. All my brethren remained for the meeting, but owing to a previous arrangement to hold Divine Service at Innisfil, nearly thirty miles from here, on my way home, I reluctantly left, and proceeded on to Bradford, eight miles, after dark, where I slept at the inn.

Jan. 20th—Reached Innisfil in good time. Held Divine Service, and preached to fifty people.

Jan. 22nd—Good congregation at Barrie. Opened a Sunday School in the church for the first time. Twenty-five children attended. A Sunday School has been at Shanty Bay since my arrival.

Jan. 24th—Walked on the ice across the Bay, a distance of two miles, to visit the settlers there. A snow storm so dreadful that it took me off my legs several times, and drove me a considerable distance along the smooth ice. Visited six families. The storm somewhat abated about five o'clock, but it was with much difficulty I was enabled to return, as the wind was against me, and the ice quite smooth, being swept completely by the wind.

Jan. 30th—Service at White's School House, Penetanguishene Road. Proceeded to Mr. Alley's, in the coloured settlement, but owing to his not having sent to the Post Office, thirteen miles off, he had not known of my going. I stopped there that night, and returned next day, riding sixteen miles in a severe storm of snow and rain.

Feb. 2nd—Walked across the Bay to visit a man who had had a severe fall from a ladder. Read and prayed with him.

Under the date of February 12th, he writes:—It is a cause of much thankfulness to me that the Church at Barrie is making rapid progress. Its state when I came was most melancholy. Almost all the members had joined other bodies, in consequence of the absence of a minister, but they are coming back. The Head of the Church is blessing my feeble exertions among them, and I have the best hopes.

March 6th—Held Divine Service at Essa School House, which was too small to hold the congregation, being above eighty. I have a hope that in some future time a church may be built in this township.

March 7th—After a funeral service at Barrie, I went to visit a sick man living a distance of fifteen miles, the rest of whose family were Romanists. Found him deplorably ignorant of the way of salvation. Read the 3rd of St. John's Gospel, and explained the only way for a sinner to be saved : concluded with prayer, in which the rest of the family joined. He was most anxious to receive the Holy Communion, but I declined administering it, as I saw he thought it would save him. On my way to Mr. Henry's, where I slept, visited a Scotch family, very respectable ; read and prayed with them. They pressed me to appoint a service to be held in the school house near ; but I fear I have too many on hand already. I purpose making some of my fortnightly meetings monthly ones, in order to occupy more stations.

March 8th—Left Mr. Alley's after breakfast, and took a circuit through Vespra ; visited several ; returned home late at night. My horse was so fagged with continual travelling, that I must give him a few days rest, which indeed I require for myself too.

March 13—Divine Service at Lake Shore.

March 14—Service at Mrs. Hall's, four miles further on. Held another service in the midst of a Scotch settlement, where I had a large congregation. I went there at the request of several persons. Did not intend keeping this up, as the place was within five miles of Orillia, where there was a missionary; however, afterwards arranged to hold service there monthly.

March 31—Held service at Innisfil: the day dreadful. Did not expect to meet any one, but was agreeably surprised with a congregation of twenty.

April 10—In consequence of the breaking up of the roads, took four hours to go eight miles to Lake Shore service.

April 11—Service at Campbell's, for first time. Intend, God willing, to continue it regularly.

April 17—Held a Vestry at Barrie: it was numerously attended. Very pleasing to see such an interest taken in the Church. Resolved to let sittings: about seventy were taken on the spot. Opened a subscription for repairs of church, and enclosing burial ground.

April 28—Did not arrive at Innisfil for an hour after time named for service, in consequence of the bad state of the roads.

Jan. 1st, 1844—The different services have been carried on regularly, but in consequence of being in an unsettled state, living in a very small house, and endeavouring to get The Parsonage forward, I have been obliged to discontinue my journal. We are now settled in The Parsonage. Went to Toronto: attended a meeting of the Church Society, and obtained from this Society a bible and two prayer books for the church at Barrie.

Jan. 16—Proceeded this day to attend the Quarterly Clerical Meeting at Mr. Osler's. Much profitable discussion on the 5th Hebrews: afterwards a long conversation on "Baptismal Regeneration"; its advocates much discomfited, and on the whole I think it was profitable, being conducted in a Christian spirit. I moved a resolution condemnatory of the Oxford principles of the "*Church*" newspaper, which was carried by the casting vote of the Chairman.

Jan. 21st—Started early for Barrie to address the children of the Sunday School, on distributing the premiums for attendance and attention, this being the anniversary of the opening of the school. Gave thirteen nice books to as many children, who seemed much gratified. The school has gone on very favourably, thank God, for the past year. Attendance here, and at Shanty Bay, small, in consequence of the severity of weather.

Jan. 22nd—Service at White's School House, afterwards at Mr. Craig's, Medonte.

Jan. 23rd—Left Mr. Craig's, and reached Mr. Raymond's School House. Had a large congregation.

Jan. 28th—Congregation at Shanty Bay, upwards of sixty.

Jan. 30th—Left Barrie early, in company with Judge Gowan. Arrived at Nottawasaga about two. Rested at a small tavern where the Judge held his Court, awaiting the erection of a suitable building, at which I gave notice of service next day at eleven.

Jan. 31st—Held service at a very neat building belonging to the Congregationalists; preached to a crowded congregation.

Feb. 18—Large congregations in Barrie and Shanty Bay; in the latter, seventy persons.

Feb. 24th—Service at Jemby's School House. Very large congregation. May His Spirit go with my humble addresses."

In September, 1844, Mr. Ardagh writes to a friend : "My time is so occupied that I have not a moment, and have to entrench on my sleeping hours for correspondence......In addition to my stations, I have been inspecting schools......... I regret to say that I am in debt; but hope, before a year, to be clear. Am obliged to borrow, to keep afloat."

For upwards of twenty-five years he held the position of Chairman of the Board of Grammar School Trustees, as well as a member and examiner of the Board of Public Instruction for the County; a body in connection with the Common School system of Upper Canada.

The following extract from his Diary will tell of his appointment as Superintendent of Schools:

"After Divine Service at Myers's School House, at Innisfil, the house being quite full, spoke to them about Schools, and gave some advice, as I was lately appointed by the unanimous vote of the Municipal Council, Superintendent of Schools for the whole County. A most responsible office. May God give me grace to discharge the duty with fidelity."

No wonder that he so acquitted himself as to become identified with the spread of education in that part of the country, and that after his death resolutions expressive of their deep sense of the value of his services should be unanimously passed, as well by the Standing Committee on Education, for the County of Simcoe, as by the Board of Public Instruction for the Northern Circuit of the same County, and by the Board of Grammar School Trustees in Barrie.

Mr. Ardagh neglected no means by which the religious and moral welfare of his flock might be forwarded. The desecration of the Sabbath openly by Sunday traffic, travelling, &c., was so lamented by him that he addressed the late Chief Justice on the subject, begging his advice and opinion as to whether the law might interfere to secure at all events its outward observance. An old newspaper of many years since reports a meeting assembled to consider the subject of temperance, at which his earnest anxiety on the subject is evident by his words. His jealousy for the honor of God in His word was fervent and strong. He even upheld that the Bible should have a foremost place in all teaching, and be its foundation-stone, and he contended zealously that the young in schools should associate their earliest remembrances with it. He also felt strongly that the Scripture should not be dishonoured by being cast out of the Common Schools, it being in his opinion a painful anomaly and disgrace that in a Christian land its schools should be deprived of God's blessed word.

Here it will be well to give a brief sketch of the progress of the Church in Mr. Ardagh's mission.

The Church Society of the Diocese of Toronto having been recently organized, Mr. Ardagh lost no time in forming a branch in Barrie, and for this purpose called a meeting on the 19th of March, 1844, which was heartily responded to by his parishioners A committee was at once formed, and a subscription list opened. So much zeal did he infuse into his people, that for many years this continued a most prosperous branch; the amount raised each year generally exceeding that of other places of even larger size: the second year the amount of subscription was nearly sixty dollars.

Mr. Ardagh's arduous labours were lightened in the autumn of 1845, by the appointment by the Bishop of a travelling missionary for the County of Simcoe, the "Parochial Association of the Simcoe District" having contributed to the funds so liberally that one-half of the stipend of a missionary (£50 sterling) could be paid from those funds." It was supplemented by £50 more from the Society itself. This formed the salary of the Rev. George Bourne, who laboured successfully for two years; but the strain proving too great for his strength, he was obliged to retire from this field of labour. He thus wrote to the Society: "I pray that the Church Society will soon be able to find a missionary who is better able to stand the fatigue of travelling, under which the strength of your first missionary is giving way"

Mr. Bourne was succeeded, in October, 1847, by the Rev. John Fletcher, who filled the same position for the next three years, and until appointed by the Bishop to an independent mission at Mono.

These clergymen were on the warmest terms of friendship with Mr Ardagh, and ever found a home at The Parsonage.

During all these years the country was becoming rapidly settled, so that Mr. Ardagh found himself quite unable to attend to the spiritual wants of his ever increasing flock. Under these circumstances he applied for assistance to the Society for the Propagation of the Gospel, and received an able and valued coadjutor in the person of the Rev Garrett Nugent, who arrived in May, 1851. Mr. Nugent was beloved and respected by all, and his departure was much regretted, when, in 1854, he returned to his native country.

The following is a letter from Mr. Ardagh to the Society for the Propagation of the Gospel, which has been copied from their published Quarterly Report, which thus introduces it :—

"The Society has recently received the following letter from a zealous clergyman in the Diocese of Toronto:

'Barrie, Canada West, March 26, 1852.

'REV. AND DEAR SIR,—I regret not having been able hitherto to comply with your request —to report as to the state of my mission of "Barrie, Shanty Bay, and *parts adjacent*," as defined in my license from the Bishop of Toronto. It is only reasonable that the venerable Society should desire to have an account of the progress made during upwards of nine years, in which I have occupied this post of duty.

'It is difficult to give even a short report without bringing the instrument into too prominent a position. On my arrival here in October, 1842, I found matters in an exceedingly discouraging state. In this district, comprising twenty-one townships, each containing an area of twelve miles square, there were but three clergymen, two of them twenty-six miles south, and east, and the third, forty miles north; while to the west all was a spiritual desert. The prospect, in every point of view, would have been disheartening, if I depended upon my own strength: There were two churches in an unfinished state, Shanty Bay and Barrie. I commenced service in them every Sunday, and selected seven stations throughout, from six to ten miles apart, where I had service once a month or fortnight. I selected them generally at a cross road or path, and in the centre of a scattered settlement. I had previously visited the people around, and enquired whether I might expect a congregation. The reply I generally received was, that if I had reference to the members of the Church, it would not be worth while to come so far, but that the people would assemble to hear any one who came as a preacher. Indeed, they were satisfied if he took his text from the Bible, and was a "smart" man; they were not particular about the doctrine. However, I continued regular services, and the congregations steadily increased; until, by degrees, many came back to the church who had left it, and expressed a wish for more frequent ministrations. In conjunction with the Rev. F. Osler, I had a resolution passed at our annual meeting of the Church Society, that our subscription should be applied toward the support of a travelling missionary, who laboured for a few years, and gave an additional monthly service to each of my stations. The desire still increased, and, in 1848, the people of my own mission offered to subscribe towards an assistant minister, to be confined within the bounds of the mission. After many difficulties in procuring one, and the disappointment by Rev. Mr. Shaw, at length Rev. G. Nugent, sent out by you, arrived here in last May. He labours most diligently, and is most acceptable to the people.

'I refrain, in this brief report, to give an account of the difficulties, trials, and hardships, inseparable from a new and bush mission. I have few instances of real conversion to relate; but the outward conformity is as great as could be expected, and God alone can, in his own good time, give the increase.

'I shall, in conclusion, merely draw the comparison between the state of the mission as I found it, and as it is at present. There are now five churches in the mission, in which Divine Service is regularly performed, besides five stations. There are three more new churches in course of erection, which, I expect, will be ready for opening before next winter. All the churches opened are furnished with books, communion plate, surplices, printed registry books, &c. In three of them there is an average congregation of from ninety to one hundred. The communicants are nearly one hundred, and increasing. A large and commodious school house has been erected in Barrie, which cost about £200, and upon which there is a debt of £70. A bell, which cost near £50, has been put up in Barrie church. When I first came, I found it difficult to raise a few pounds for church purposes; for instance, it took three years to pay for the painting of the *outside* of Barrie church. In the last year the sum of £133 was raised in that village alone for church purposes. The mission subscribes £75 per annum for the assistant minister, besides what is sent to the Church Society. The £100 generously granted to my mission, and the £16 which came through your Society, I have divided between four churches and the school house in Barrie. This school house has been used for Divine Service, by the Bishop's permission, on Sunday nights, during the winter, as the church being situated on the top of a steep hill, it was impracticable for old persons and children to go up there after night, by reason of snow and ice. This evening service in Barrie, makes five full services in the mission every Sunday. Besides the stations I have mentioned, the travelling missionary and I held an occasional service in the township of St. Vincent, eighty miles from this, for the more particular purpose of baptizing the children of the new settlers, and keeping our people from straying; and on one occasion I went as far as Owen Sound, one hundred and twenty miles distant. A clergyman having been settled in this latter place in 1849, he has taken that distant part of the mission off my hands. Another station to the east has, by the Bishop's arrangement, been handed over to the clergyman at Orillia, so that this mission is now reduced to about thirty miles square. I should observe that the new churches are only externally completed, but they present a neat ecclesiastical appearance, with Gothic windows, &c. Some English gentlemen, in travelling through my mission, expressed their agreeable surprise in meeting such in so remote and wild a country.

They still want pulpit, reading desk, and sittings. At present we are satisfied with a table borrowed from a neighbouring house as a substitute for the former, and are contented with planks set on blocks of wood for the latter. We were forced to occupy them thus early, as the school house had become too small for the congregations, and we were occasionally interfered with by others who had an equal right to their use. The resources of the people have been well nigh exhausted in getting the churches thus far; and being now obliged to subscribe towards a minister's stipend, they require a little breathing time. If those friends at home who may read this imperfect sketch, would contribute something to their completion, it would be most gratefully accepted. I should like to have them all completed before I remove to a more settled place, as it is probable that I shall have to apply to the Bishop before long for this favour. I find my physical powers failing, and am unable to take those long rides on horseback which I have hitherto done.

"My health broke down in 1849, and I had to go to England to seek for its renewal, as well as to transact some private affairs. I suffered from rheumatism in the head, contracted from sleeping in shanties imperfectly protected from the weather. My visit home has considerably restored me, but I yet feel the increase of years by stiffness of the limbs, &c.

"I hope that this imperfect outline will satisfy the venerable Society that some progress has been made. I have reason to think that my venerable and energetic Bishop is satisfied with me. All I can say is, that I have endeavoured to set forth Christian truth before the people, as is contained in the articles, homilies, and offices of our beloved Church.

"In fine, I trust it is my highest object to look forward to the time, when, through Divine grace, I may be permitted to hear from the lips of the Chief Shepherd, 'Well done, thou faithful servant; enter thou into the joy of thy Lord.'

"Yours in the best bonds,
"S. B. ARDAGH."

In the summer of 1847, Mr. Ardagh was much affected by hearing of the death of his wife's brother, the Rev. Richard Anderson, Incumbent of New Ireland, Province of Quebec. This devoted clergyman had been sent by the Bishop to take a week's duty, in rotation with other clergymen, in ministering to the wants of the poor emigrants in the Quarantine sheds of Grosse Isle. The emigrant fever was sweeping them off by hundreds, and nurses could not be obtained, so he remained for five weeks longer, doing his Master's work, and, finally at His feet, laid down his life, in obedience to the Divine command, "Ye ought also to lay down your lives for the brethren."

His constitution had been already undermined by grief for the death of his young wife, the preceding year; and his strength was so completely prostrated by these six weeks of arduous labour, that he returned to Quebec stricken with the fever, to which he succumbed.

His mortal remains now lie with those of two more devoted fellow labourers* in the same work, in the Cemetery at Quebec.

Mr. Ardagh at once proceeded to the Lower Province, to bring back with him his two little orphan nephews, and Miss Anderson, who had been supplying the place of mother to them From this time they were to him as his own children. The elder, Richard, met with a sad fate, being drowned by falling through the ice on Kempenfeldt Bay, when only nine years old The younger, James, survived his adopted father but three months. Always exemplary in his life, and of remarkable sweetness of character, he had before him a happy prospect for this world—having been but three months married to an amiable and affectionate wife. But it pleased Providence that it should be otherwise; for after a short and painful illness he entered

---

* The Rev. Mr. Morris and Rev. Mr. Chatterton. The wife of the latter generously erected a handsome iron railing, enclosing the three graves.

with peace and hope into the kingdom of His Father, on the 13th January, 1870.

The winter of 1847-48, brought Mr. Ardagh the heaviest trouble of his life. His beloved wife, after many years of patient suffering, was nearing the end of her earthly pilgrimage. The great influence she exercised over him, in every way, has already been noticed. To the graces of her intellect and character ample testimony has been borne, as well by the friends of her early youth, as by those of her later life. She was one of those whose memory is blessed by her children. The late revered Bishop of Toronto, Dr. Strachan, a man of great penetration, to whom she was well known, said of her many years after her departure hence, that "one equally good and gifted he had never met." One who met her for the first time, after her arrival in this country, writes of her thus: "His gifted and sainted wife was to her husband a tower of strength, and few persons had more to struggle against; great delicacy of health, difficulties in a new country which can be easily imagined, a large family, and very limited means. Notwithstanding this, a generous hospitality and a kindly welcome greeted as well the chance visitor as the intimate friend, and in the domestic circle her cares were unceasing for those whose stay and comfort she ever was; she lived hardly six years after her arrival in Canada, but it was long enough to surround her with an atmosphere of love."

Under her loving influence the impetuous, and, at times, unconsidered judgment of her husband, became sobered and matured—a more than ordinary tact supplied that which was lacking in him. His later sermons were filled with more spiritual earnestness than those of his earlier years, and he learned to look forward, with assurance of hope, to that better country where the Christian course is marked by no deviation, and where the peace which passes understanding is realised in the unclouded brightness of the Saviour's presence.

For many months her mind was filled with unutterable anguish at the thought of her husband left desolate by the loss of her love and prayerful counsel, and of her seven children bereft in early youth of a mother's watchful guidance; at the last, however, she was enabled to cast the burden of her anxieties on Him, whom, from her youth up, she had earnestly endeavoured to serve.

She entered into rest on the 4th March, 1848, without a cloud—except her bodily suffering—to mar the brightness of her departure.*

At this time Mr. Ardagh's ministerial duties were of such an arduous and absorbing nature as to leave him but small leisure for painful thought. He felt for a time, with exceeding anxiety, the great weight of responsibility which devolved upon him as father of a young and motherless family, to whom he could give but comparatively small care, on account of the all-engrossing work of his sacred profession.

His simple faith overcame this pressing trouble. He prayed for them earnestly and unceasingly, assembling, at times, the elder ones for special appeals to the Throne of Grace; and confided them altogether to the care of Him who is the great bearer of burdens. Towards the close of his life he often spoke with deep gratitude of his answered prayers, inasmuch as none of his children had ever caused him anxiety or distress of mind on their account.

---

* It is desired here to record an act of faithful friendship on the part of Mrs. O'Brien, of "The Woods," then residing in Toronto, who hastened, in inclement weather and almost impassable roads, to aid and comfort the family of her departed friend, by whom she was always beloved and revered.

Reference has just been made to the character of Mr. Ardagh's work at this time. He was strenuously exerting himself to extend the Church's influence in the neighborhood of Barrie. A circular on this subject, bearing his signature, was published in a local newspaper, and will show how deeply he felt his responsibility as a minister in a new country, and how anxious he was to provide for the spiritual wants of those who were perishing for lack of knowledge.

This letter appeared in a Barrie newspaper, under date of January 7th, 1848:—

"*To the Members of the United Church of England and Ireland, in the neighbourhood of Barrie:*

"My Dear Brethren,—From conversations I have had with several persons, I find that much misunderstanding prevails with respect to the project lately put forth at our public meetings, for increasing the ministrations of the Church in the neighbourhood of Barrie I purpose to address some more meetings on the same subject, shortly, and should have done so before this, but for a melancholy event in my family.

"Allow me, therefore, through the medium of our local press, to explain an object which I have much at heart, and which I trust will commend itself to every true member of the Church to which it is our happiness to belong.

"When I came to this country, about five years since, I found that extensive spiritual destitution prevailed, and that but for the occasional preaching of the ministers of other bodies of Christians, the benefits of which I here most readily acknowledge, a state of things bordering upon heathenism must soon have pervaded the mass of the community.

"I immediately commenced religious services on *week days*, at as many convenient places as my time permitted; the Sundays being occupied by two services. But the more I did, the more I found necessary to be done. At length the Rev. Mr. Osler, with a similar feeling, joined me in making application to the Church Society for assistance towards the support of a travelling missionary for the entire district, and we pledged ourselves to raise by subscription a certain sum. We succeeded, and many of you can testify to the great usefulness of that missionary. But what could one clergyman effect in so extensive a field? His duties were so onerous, that he was, after a short time, as you are aware, obliged to give up.

"Under these circumstances, and finding that the increasing population of Barrie began to occupy more of my time, I thought it advisable to take another step in advance, namely, to recommend to my flock to subscribe towards the maintenance of an assistant minister for this immediate neighbourhood, one of us to reside in Barrie.

"My object is simply to form, as it were, a large

parish, say from twelve to fifteen miles around the town of Barrie, and in that to have about six regular stations, two of which might be occupied every Sunday, and thus to give each a Sunday service every third week, as also an intervening service on the week-day, when the minister could visit from house to house, an important duty, which is now, from necessity, almost neglected.

From the assurances of support I have already received, I have taken upon me the responsibility of inviting a clergyman from the old country. I therefore call upon you to relieve me from the anxiety which that responsibility involves.

The members of my congregation in Barrie have set a good example: so cordially did they enter into my views, that they have already pledged themselves to give upwards of forty pounds a year, and this in addition to a contribution towards my own support, in the shape of pew rents. I beg to impress upon you a few facts:—1st. That more than one-half of your present minister's support is derived from the voluntary subscriptions of the people of England. 2nd. That our Church receives no support from Government. 3rd. That the Clergy Reserves are only sufficient as yet to support a few clergymen, in the entire Province. 4th. That even under these circumstances, I have never yet asked or received any support from you. I am therefore emboldened to lay upon you a conscientious duty,—that of supplying yourselves with the ministrations of religion, without which no blessing can rest upon you or your families. It is indeed gratifying to observe an anxiety to build churches to assemble in, but of what use is this, if the sound of the gospel is not to be heard in them? All that is wanting is the will and a united effort, as I know that the number of professing members is sufficient to accomplish much more.

Adopting, then, the language of the Bishop of Montreal, I would say—"It is time for you to recognize the principles, and practically to own the claims of your church. Scattered as you are among other religious denominations, and incorporated in the civil relations of life, that, surely, is no reason why you should yourselves be backward in zeal for your church. Breathing the spirit of love to all around you, you must trust that those who do not agree with you, will never quarrel with you for being attached to your own principles; and even if they would, you must remember that you have a cause to support, a faith for which to contend, a sacred and treasured system of religion to transmit to the "generations to come—that your posterity may know it, and the children which are yet unborn, to the intent that when they come up, they may teach their children the same." The day has arrived in which the growing wants of the church can no longer be supplied exclusively by drawing from sources which lie at a distance: the supply must spring forth, and that freely, from the soil, or much of the rising growth will wither at the root. It is impossible to suppose that we can go on for ever in this dependent condition, adding burden to burden, year after year, to those already undertaken by our generous friends on the other side of the Atlantic. In fact, it is now distinctly expected from us, in that quarter, that we should make some vigorous effort for ourselves. Look, then, and with an unshrinking eye, at your position. Consider the responsibilities which devolve upon you. Assume your task with hope and gladness of mind. Confide it to God in the name of his blessed Son. Remember with thankfulness to Him how dear your church ought to be to your hearts, and how imperative is her claim upon your undivided allegiance and support. A church who builds her faith upon the pure word of God, and is behind no body of believers in the proclamation of Christ crucified, as the sole hope of sinners, and the strenuous assertion in all points, of "the truth as it is in Jesus;" a church in our own day extending far and wide over the world,—carrying the lamp of the gospel, not only to the limits of the empire, but also into the darkened abodes of heathens and Jews; spreading also with an almost unparalleled rapidity in that branch which subsists in a neighbouring Republic.

God forbid, that in thus speaking, we should mean to promote a hollow reliance upon external privileges alone, or a disdain of other Christian bodies. We do not mean to say that the church has no imperfections, or that her light has never waxed dull; and as for ourselves, clerical and lay members, we have faults and sins enough among us to keep the lessons of humility and fear before our eyes. What I speak of is, our *duty* to our church,—a duty arising from our privileges,—the calls upon us in proportion to our blessings; and truly I fear it must humble rather than exalt us in our own sight, if we ask whether we have fully responded to these calls. This church is planted among us—shall we keep and shall we cherish our religious inheritance, and seek to pass it down to our children?—or shall we suffer it to languish and decay? These are questions which must be answered by our deeds as well as by our professions; and, God be praised, we have made a *beginning*. Here, then, let me call upon you as Christians and as churchmen—admitting no thought of failure in my appeal—to come forward and do your part; remembering the command laid upon you "to honor the Lord with your substance, and with the first fruits of all your increase—as persons owing a debt of gratitude to the church in the mother country; stimulated by her example, to remember the words of the Lord Jesus—" Freely ye have received, freely give," and that question of the Apostle,—"If we have sown unto you spiritual things, is it a great matter if we reap your carnal things?" I might add much more, but I forbear; and though I might be bold in Christ to enjoin that which is convenient, yet for love's sake I rather beseech your co-operation in this important matter. I have consecrated this the first day of the new year to this solemn appeal. God grant that it may have its due effect; and that the year we have been graciously permitted to commence, may teem with spiritual and temporal blessings on you all, is the sincere prayer of your affectionate servant in Christ,

S. B. ARDAGH.

P.S.—I here subjoin a heading for the subscription list, in the hope that some will undertake to have it filled up in each locality.

We, the undersigned, do pledge ourselves to pay annually the sums attached to our names, to the church-wardens of Barrie, for the time being, for the support of an Assistant Minister to the Rev. S. B. Ardagh, and to continue the same for at least three years: the first payment to be made on the 1st January, 1849.

In his doctrinal views Mr. Ardagh, belonged to that school which is commonly called Evangelical: in other words, he accepted and interpreted the articles of our church in the same sense as those who had framed them. Of him it may be truly said that he preached in all their fulness those great truths for which our reformers did not think their lives too dear a price, for the sake of which alone it was worth either effecting or preserving a reformation. But while strenuously opposing all tendency to Romish error, he was staunch in his attachment to the catholic ritual and primitive constitution of the church to which he belonged. In every consistent Christian he recognized a brother, but his charity never for one moment rendered him disloyal to his own principles as a churchman As a champion of all that he believed true he was bold and fearless No motives of policy or expediency, no fear of man deterred him for a moment from expressing himself as the occasion required. Being in a minority, or even single-handed, made no difference to him when on the side of what he felt to be right,—and hence, in a large degree, may be explained the high respect which was entertained for him by men of all varieties of religious opinion The *Echo*, a paper devoted to the spread of evangelical truth, and following in the footsteps of the *Berean*, (a Christian journal long published in the diocese of Quebec, but then no longer extant,) was originated by him in conjunction with his deeply valued friends, the Very Rev. Dean Grasett, the Rev. Canon Baldwin, and others. He supported this publication with his pen and his purse to the utmost of his ability In this, as in other matters, he asked continually for the blessing and assistance of his Heavenly Master.

It has been intimated that the subject of this memoir was accustomed to take an active part in the proceedings of Synod. In that assembly, the views of Mr. Ardagh were, unfortunately, as the writer thinks, by no means popular: and occasionally it happened that on questions which he deemed of great importance he found himself in a small minority. That under such circumstances he always acted with a sound discretion is more perhaps than can be said with truth. His feelings being deeply interested he could not invariably express himself with the calmness and moderation to be observed in some. But while he never hesitated, sometimes with undue impetuosity, to speak out his mind, it was so evident that he spoke from his heart and without bitterness, that he always managed to avoid giving offence. Though there was no man perhaps in the Synod whose outspoken sentiments were more opposed to those of the clergy in general, it may be safely said that there was no one who was so general a favourite with all parties.

As a speaker, Mr. Ardagh possessed considerable power, and never failed to convey his meaning to all around, though it may be that he was wanting in some of the attractions which at once arrest the attention of a popular assembly. He never electrified his hearers by sudden flashes of eloquence, or carried them away in a torrent of impassioned declamation But, on the other hand, he never startled them by paradox, or offended them by bombast. On one occasion only did the writer of these lines enjoy the privilege of hearing him preach ; and it is scarcely fair to judge from a single sermon. He has, however, no hesitation in saying that that particular sermon was one of the best he ever listened to ; and from what he has heard from others he has little doubt that, as a preacher, Mr. Ardagh was even more distinguished than as a speaker. The newspaper report of him, after his death, speaks of his preaching as being marked by that simple yet expressive style, which found its way to the heart, which is perhaps the best praise which can possibly be given to any pulpit oratory.

The following anonymous letter, received by Mr. Ardagh, in March, 1869, cheered him much, and encouraged him to the hope that the words of life had not been spoken in vain :—

"REV. SIR.—Since hearing that on account of declining health, you are prohibited by your medical advisers from preaching to us any more, I cannot resist an inclination I feel to address you. Although, sir, I know that as your afflictions abound, your consolation must also abound; still, sir, I think that after a long life spent in preaching the gospel it must be cheering to find that you have not spent your strength for nought. Such, dear sir, is my apology for writing you a few lines. I consider it to be my duty, having for some time sat under your ministry, to bear my humble testimony in the fear of God to your unceasing—and especially of late, as you no doubt felt the day approaching—earnestness to declare unto us the whole counsel of God, and that so plainly that even the weakest comprehension amongst us could not by any means mistake you.

"You have faithfully given forth no uncertain sound, but have preached to us none but Jesus You have told us that there is no salvation in any other, none but Christ, no unnecessary rites of man's invention, nothing in short but the simple faith of the Bible; and, sir, I can testify—after closely following you—that if any of your hearers are lost, their blood will be upon their own heads; for you have at all times declared unto us that unless we believe, and rest entirely upon the merits of Christ, we cannot be saved.

"Praying that the consolations you so well expressed in a sermon 'Even to your old age I am He; and to hoar hairs I will carry you,' may be richly experienced by yourself,

"I beg to subscribe myself,

"A BENEFITED HEARER IN
TRINITY CHURCH, BARRIE."

As years went on Mr. Ardagh found his strength for the work of visiting his people gradually diminishing, and his distance from most of them was always a serious hindrance in the way of seeing them. He did, however, what he could in this direction, feeling deeply the immense importance of confirming in private what he taught in public, and there is good reason for believing that his visits were always greatly appreciated, and very especially by the sick. It may be asserted that very few clergymen could shew as much work done in a similar space of time. Mr. Ardagh, coming to this country in the prime of life, full of vigor, filled with zeal, sanguine as to results, pursued his missionary labours with such utter disregard of health and personal comfort that after a few years his strength succumbed. Long attacks of fainting and subsequent exhaustion compelled him to cease from work for a time, and in 1849 he returned to his native country, accompanied by his eldest daughter, to recruit his health

While there he acted as one of a church deputation in the interests of a religious society, travelling and holding meetings throughout the North of Ireland. Setting sail from Liverpool to return home after an absence of seven months they encountered such severe gales, as narrowly to escape shipwreck, the ship being driven under bare poles four hundred miles back to Cork, where the vessel put in to refit. They eventually reached home in February, 1850.

During his absence death had again visited his household, his mother-in-law having, at the advanced age of upwards of ninety years, joyfully accepted her emancipation from the bondage of age and infirmity. This venerable woman who had survived her own large family, with the exception of one unmarried daughter, had resided with him during the entire period of his married life. The relation between them had always been characterized by perfect harmony of opinion and warmth of affection. She died on 1st June, 1849.

From the time of Mr. Nugent's departure in 1854, for a period of about eighteen months, Mr. Ardagh was without assistance.

Rev. Edward Morgan visited Canada in 1854 to recruit his health, impaired by years of ministerial labour in the West Indies. The result of this visit was his decision to accept the post of assistant minister at Barrie. He returned from the island of St. Vincent with his family in the autumn of 1855 to settle finally in Barrie. Mr. Morgan's opinions in the matter of faith and doctrine were identical with those of Mr. Ardagh, and, during the fourteen years in which they labored together, they were in perfect accord and unity. Mr. Ardagh found in Mr. Morgan a faithful friend and earnest co-adjutor, and spoke of him to the last hours of his life with affection and respect.

Mr. Ardagh had before this time been convinced that Barrie, as the centre of his labours, should be his place of residence. Barrie was the county town, and had increased greatly in population, and was obviously the place to which, apart from its being the rectory, the ministratrations of a clergyman should be confined.

We have stated the reasons why Shanty Bay became Mr. Ardagh's home. Having spent all the means he had upon the parsonage there, it was not in his power to build another house. His diary mentions the letting of sittings in Barrie church. The first receipts from these, Mr. Ardagh returned as a contribution towards painting and repairing the church, then much in need of renovation. The church, being built upon glebe lands, the pew rents formed part of the endowment. After some years these lands gradually acquired value, the income for the last two years being probably as much as for the first ten years of his incumbency. Just before the last serious illness of Mr. Ardagh he had made up his mind to come to Barrie, as he more and more felt his inability to visit his flock in and around Barrie as often as he wished. This step was not contemplated without a pang at the prospect of leaving the quiet and pretty home, the scene of so many joys and sorrows. To this old place the attachment of himself and his children was very great. During these years the fund attached to the Shanty Bay mission gradually diminished, and in the end was wholly lost by reason of the failure of the Bank of Upper Canada, in the stock of which institution the fund was invested.

We have to record here another sad incident connected with this period of Mr. Ardagh's life: the death of Arthur, the youngest of his twin sons. He was a young man of much promise, and had chosen the law for his profession, of which he was a diligent and devoted student.

Naturally of a delicate constitution, but of indefatigable industry, he pursued his legal and other studies to the serious injury of his health. In the spring of 1854 he ruptured a blood vessel, the alarming symptom of an insidious disease, the fatal tendency of which became evident as autumn approached. His anxious father felt it his duty to accede to the advice of his physician to send the invalid to a warmer climate, in the vain hope of prolonging a valued life. The latter patiently acquiesced in what was thought best for him, and reluctantly left the loved and loving home he was never to see again.

He was accompanied by his eldest sister as nurse and companion, their destination being Aiken, South Carolina, a secluded village situated in a pine forest, considered a salubrious resort for invalids. Arriving as strangers they made many friends among these warm-hearted southern people, and were the recipients of numberless acts of kindness and sympathy. Three months afterwards he was attacked by the last fatal symptoms; and, with perfect calmness, he received the intimation that his days were numbered. His faith and trust were on a sure foundation; and, throughout his illness, no murmur or complaint ever passed his lips. His love and gratitude to the sister who never left him were unbounded. On the morning of his death—having dressed as carefully as if he were going for a walk—he turned to her and said : " Dear E , will you come with me ?" "Where, love ?" "Through the dark valley." "I cannot, darling ; but Jesus will." She then repeated the 23rd Psalm, in which he fervently joined. Then he said : "I think I'll lie down ;"

which he did, and fell into a quiet slumber, from which he never woke. Without even a sigh, his happy spirit left the worn-out body, for the everlasting rest above, on the 12th January, 1855.

Truly the prayers of the good father and mother were answered; and the end of their son was perfect peace. With them he now worships around the Throne. The sorrowing sister found a temporary home with her kind and Christian friends, the Rev. Mr. and Mrs. Cornish. He had been unremitting in his ministerial visits to the invalid, and did everything that Christian sympathy could suggest to mitigate the sorrow of such a time.

The sorrow-stricken father proceeded at once to bring home his daughter, left lonely in a strange land. They left all that was mortal of the beloved son and brother in the peaceful churchyard of Aiken, nearly a thousand miles from home.

Early in the year 1857, Mr. Ardagh again crossed the Atlantic in search of health, and at this time visited the Continent of Europe, as well as England, Scotland, and Ireland.

His love for the beautiful was amply gratified during this prolonged course of travel, and is recorded in many sparkling descriptions touching upon the old glories and sacred associations of Rome, the sunny beauty of the Bay of Naples, and the blended loveliness and sublimity of Swiss mountains and lakes

Any extracts from his letters would be out of place here, touching, as they do, on subjects made familiar by the eloquent pens of many tourists

---

The next incident which demands notice in this brief record is Mr. Ardagh's second marriage; which took place on the 9th December, 1859.

He had been a widower for a period of nearly twelve years, during which time his three eldest daughters had married and left the paternal home. The lady upon whom his choice fell was Helena, fourth daughter of William Durie, Esq., K. H., sometime of the Ordnance Medical Department Well, indeed, did she justify the prudence of a step which, in the case of a clergyman, has so great an effect upon his usefulness.

Her Christian deportment and congenial and affectionate disposition added much brightness to his declining years. "Often," says one who knew Mrs. Ardagh well, "have I heard him speak in his last illness of the happiness of his married life, saying that never was man so blessed in companions, for the equals of his first and second wives could scarcely be met with, and so," he adds, "think those who knew them both."

That she was beloved and appreciated by all his family was a source of great happiness to him. For this, as for all other blessings which surrounded his path in his later years, he was devoutly and unceasingly thankful.

For many years a Grammar School had been flourishing at Barrie under the care of the Rev. William F. Checkley, B. A., a gentlemen whose rare and distinguished scholarship was surpassed, if possible, by anxiety to do all the good within his power.

From him Mr. Ardagh was accustomed to receive much valuable help, which he appreciated the more as Mr. Checkley's theological views coincided with his own. It so happened, however, that, in 1861, Mr. Checkley was appointed rector of the Model Grammar School, Toronto; but at the end of two years he was again occupying his old position at Barrie, the Government grant for the support of the school at Toronto having been suddenly withdrawn. It was fortunate for Mr. Ardagh that at the time he most needed help it was again generously supplied to him by his old friend. In the summer of 1861 he was reminded, by a serious attack of illness, that he was no longer equal to the severe labours which had distinguished his earlier years; and though, after a time, he recovered so far as to take an active part in the working of his parish, yet from this time he was compelled to moderate his exertions, and to be more careful of his health.

In 1864 a new and much larger church was built at Barrie, the old structure having become altogether inadequate to the wants of that thriving town. Nor were church matters at Shanty Bay at this time stationary. The interior arrangements had been altered to afford increased accommodation; and, in 1854, Mr. Ardagh's younger daughters (who always took a most loving interest in this church) collected a large sum, with which a fine bell, costing about $400, was purchased, also complete new hangings, matting, blinds, &c. One member of the congregation gave a carpet for the chancel; others also contributed liberally to the furnishing of the church.

Greater exertions daily became necessary for the due discharge of his ministerial functions, and these were times when a sense of his growing weakness occasioned him no little uneasiness.

But faith in God was one of Mr. Ardagh's characteristics; and now, as always, did he "cast his burden upon the Lord."

To some extent his lack of service was supplied by his assistant the Rev. E. Morgan (now his worthy successor as Rector of Barrie.)

The sphere of this gentleman's duties lay outside of Barrie; but, in addition, he undertook others in the town itself where he resided, and thus afforded to Mr. Ardagh a grateful and almost necessary relief from labours which, year by year, were pressing upon him more heavily.

In 1867, he accepted the Rural Deanery of Simcoe, the offer of which was made to him by the Bishop, as he was the senior clergyman, and on account of the "zeal and activity" he had shewn as Chairman of the branch of the Society in that district.

We here append a portion of a letter written since his death by an old friend and brother clergyman, Dr. O'Meara, Rector of Port Hope:—

"I have," writes the Doctor, "the most pleasant recollections of a missionary journey that Mr. A. and myself made some years ago to the Muskoka territory. He was at the time in very bad health, and the weather was more than usuallly inclement. Many younger men would have pleaded ill health as a reason for not fulfilling the arduous duties which the authorities of the Diocese had laid on him; but he refused to avail himself of that plea, and completed the whole programme of meetings and services, preaching and speaking with all the fervor and earnestness that had marked him when a much younger and quite healthy man.

"On that tour a very delicate task fell to him quite unexpectedly. He was called on after a Sunday service to mediate between a clergyman of his rural deanery and a discontented and complaining congregation; and I remember being much pleased with the tact and faithfulness which he manifested in dealing with the difficulty."

But the time now was fast approaching when his term of service would be over; nor could the utmost efforts of affection prevail to put it off. In the summer of 1868 a return of acute suffering, caused by a complicated disorder of the liver, obliged him once more to place himself under medical treatment, and he was advised that the only thing to save his life, even through the approaching winter, was a sea voyage, followed by entire cessation from labour. When this sad announcement was made to his congregation at Barrie, they lost no time in presenting him with a handsome purse to defray the expenses.

The following letter from his old and esteemed parishioner Edmund S. Lally, Esq., accompanied the purse :—

MY DEAR SIR.—The late hour at which Mrs. Lally has returned from her collecting tour (11 p.m.), and the necessity for mailing this to-night, is the only apology I can offer for its not being accompanied by a suitable address to you on your departure. Your own kind heart will, I am sure, suggest all that we would have desired to say on such an occasion.

With our united kind remembrances to Mrs. Ardagh, and sincere wishes for your speedy and complete restoration to health,

I remain, dear sir,

Yours very truly.

EDMUND S. LALLY.

Hasty arrangements were made with regard to Mr. Ardagh's duty; and once more he crossed the Atlantic in the spring of 1868. The sea voyage and the subsequent care and devoted watchfulness of his brother-in-law, Dr. Edward Long, of Dublin, tended for a time to the temporary amelioration of his malady, and the great increase of his bodily ease.

It was the opinion of Dr. Long, however, corroborated by Dr. Hudson, of Dublin, and afterwards confirmed by Dr. Gull, of London, that the constitution was completely broken up, and that his life could not be much prolonged. His beloved wife, who ministered to him with untiring affection, could not bring herself to believe that such was the case, his sufferings being so much abated, and in consequence all his natural brightness of spirit having returned to him. He, however, was not deceived. In October of that year he thus wrote to one of his children in allusion to the death of a little grandson: "I can in imagination see the four carrying the little coffin up the hill, and the vault opening again to receive another. It will not be long till I add to the number already there. I wish my coffin to be placed over that of your dear mother."

After leaving Dublin Mr. Ardagh visited his youngest daughter, wife of Capt. E. C. C. Foster, of the 12th regiment, then stationed at Plymouth, where he spent some very happy days, rambling about Mount Edgecumbe, visiting Torquay and the many objects of interest in the neighbourhood. His daughter, in recalling this time, spoke of the great shock which she experienced in noticing his altered appearance and increased feebleness, notwithstanding which his chivalrous and unselfish devotion always manifested to his wife and daughters, had not in any degree relaxed.

Some months later he made a long and fatiguing voyage in very stormy weather from Dublin to Plymouth for the purpose of baptizing her first-born child.

When in London Mr. Ardagh was frequently and hospitably entertained by the Rev. Henry Stebbing, D.D., Rector of St. James's, Hampstead Road, and his accomplished wife. This gentleman, who was a connection of Mr. Ardagh's first wife, and in whose society he had passed many happy days in his earlier life, found leisure from engrossing literary work to amuse and cheer his invalid friend during his short residence in London.

During this summer he had the pleasure of spending a few days with Lady Brydges, of Boultibrooke, Radnorshire, a friend and former parishioner of his, and also with Lady Wetherall, a cousin of his wife's, whose distinguished husband met with so untimely an end some months later. He also visited his venerable uncle, Col. Ardagh, of Taunton, Somersetshire, who has since passed away.

At Coolaghmore House, Kilkenny, the residence of Mr. and Mrs. Weld, where he spent some happy days, he had the great pleasure of meeting another aged uncle, Stephen Russell Ardagh, of Callan, the last surviving brother of his father, and the father of Mrs. Weld and of his son-in-law, William D. Ardagh.

His letters also speak of the hospitality and kindness of many other friends and relatives: his beloved friend of early days, Rev. Arthur Moneypeny, Vicar of Bally-James-Duff, Rev. Henry Stewart, son-in-law of his old friend Archdeacon Palmer, of Guelph, Rev. Mr. Greene, Rector of Granard, whose wife is sister of one whom he warmly valued, Judge Gwynne, of Toronto, his brother-in-law. At Pouldrew House, County Waterford, he was cordially welcomed by the family of Richard Power, Esq., who was then in Canada, and who has lately made this country his home.

At this time, though separated from his people, he was with them in spirit, as was apparent by frequent allusions to them in his letters. On one occasion he writes "The only trouble I have is, about my services at home. I must leave this in God's hands. He knows how anxious I am about them." An effort was made to induce him to spend the winter in England; but his heart yearned after his family and his people; and feeling that his days were numbered, he longed earnestly to return. and die amongst them.

Mr. Ardagh returned to Canada in November; but from that time he was never able to do more than take an occasional service, and even that sorely tried his failing strength.

It was said of him, "the darkest shadow which dimmed his bright spirit, arose from the thought of his uselessness in his Master's service, and throughout his long illness, when he felt at all able, nothing could prevent his using his slight accession of strength in the exercise of his duty." One who can best testify, knows that in the quiet of his chamber his prayers were constantly offered up for his people.

Mr. Ardagh's only unmarried daughter, of whom he said that her faithful love and tenderness were an inexpressible solace to him, thus writes of her father : "For many years past he had been accustomed to assemble round his table, every New Year's day his numerous family connections. This always afforded him extreme pleasure, he was never happier than when surrounded by those he loved, and seemed to find his own enjoyment in the quiet contemplation of the happiness of others. On the last New Year's day of his life, he desired that there should be no departure from this custom ; but there seemed many obstacles in the way—the feebleness of his health, the severity of the weather, and other circumstances seemed to combine to render it difficult for all to meet. Those of his family still left at home tried by every means to dissuade him from thinking of it, fearing that he was unequal to the exertion, but he would not listen to the suggestion of any difficulties. He said cheerfully, though a little sadly, that it would be his last New Year's day on earth, and it would be a great disappointment to him if he could not have the pleasure of seeing those he loved so fondly once more gathered round him. To others he said he was sure they would not disappoint him when he had set his heart on it; his wish was gratified, and those who saw him that day will not soon forget the sweet and happy expression of his patient face. He took his usual place at the dinner table, and though he could not eat a morsel of food, he by no sign betrayed that he was weak and suffering; but was, as always, watchful and anxious that every one should be well attended to; he expressed his pleasure at seeing the circle assembled once more; and spoke in loving terms of the only absent one, who was divided from him by the wide Atlantic. During the whole evening his face and manner showed to us, who watched him, that he was becoming daily more chastened and purified from earthly dross. We fancied we could already see the bright reflection of the Father's face, that even then he had in view the glorious inheritance of the saints in light."*

In June, 1869, he attended Synod for the last time, but though he listened with interest to

---

* The circumstances of that evening suggested the following verses to one of his sons-in-law. When written they were read aloud to the group assembled. He for whom they were penned listening with grateful look of happy assent:

"The evening hour glides softly towards me,
  In blended lines of light and shade,
Fair as a morn of mist and gladness.
  Albeit in solemn garb arrayed.

All perfumed by the love around me.
  The twilight deepens into night;
Morn's colors brightly still surround me,
  The reflex of departed light.

While tender arms are round me twining,
  The vesper calm glides sweetly by,
In deepest peace my soul enshrining,
  As closes Life's brief history.

And yet though heart and strength are failing,
  With earthly beauty, love, and light.
No doubt of HIM my soul assailing
  Hath added darkness to the night.

Is there not love, and light, and beauty
  Where blackness broods with ebon plume;
A morning star, a dawning glory,
  To light the shadows of the tomb.

Yes, in the lore of sacred story
  Are found the records of that shore,
To which the Lamb's love and His glory,
  Doth light the path for evermore.

And so may twilight blend with darkness,
  For living love in deathless band,
My Saviour's love is cast around me.
  And naught can snatch me from His hand."

some of the debates, he made no attempt to take any part in them, a fact itself significant of failing powers, if the same thing were not sadly apparent to his brethren from his strangely altered appearance. Probably there were few who met him on that occasion who did not feel that his kind and venerable face would never be seen among them again. Speedily, indeed, were the forebodings realized of those who were most shocked at beholding him a mere wreck of his former self; for within a month he, with difficulty, managed to preach his last sermon. "The 11th of July," writes Mrs. Ardagh, "was the last Sunday he proclaimed the everlasting Gospel to his congregation at Shanty Bay, where he had faithfully preached it for nearly 27 years. The Rev. Mr. Morgan being obliged to be absent on that day, he undertook the whole service, but being unequal to the delivery of a sermon, he made a few observations extempore, in the reading desk, from the 2nd lesson of the day: 1 Thess. 3rd chap. A feeling of extreme nervousness was experienced through the church when he commenced, all knowing how unequal he was to the exertion. But it seemed as if he felt that his days here were but few, and that the place wherein he stood would soon know him no more, for with all his heart's earnest breathings, as if with the Spirit's power, he spoke of the unsearchable riches of Christ, and of the full pardon promised to all sinners believing in his blessed name; praying his hearers to remember all he had said to them, and to accept the offer of salvation while it was called to-day, "building up themselves in their most holy faith, praying in the Holy Ghost, and looking for the mercy of our Lord Jesus Christ unto eternal life"

He was much affected, his voice, at times, betraying his emotion. While in the church the same feeling was audibly manifested by his hearers.

The writer adds, "May they with God's blessing, during his long ministry of holy things, have turned many feet into the path of peace, proving to them a well of life. May he not have labored in vain; that at the coming of our Lord Jesus Christ, with all His saints, we might meet and dwell together, an acceptable people, for ever with the Lord, in the joys of immortality. He has often said that he never preached a sermon without saying, even in a few words, that which might, by the grace of God, save a soul—'Jesus is the way, the truth, and the life.' This was the substance of his advice, as regards preaching, to many a young brother in the ministry. Oh! may many souls be given to him as his rejoicing in that day when God shall make up his jewels."

In the same month, also, he preached his last sermon in Barrie. Knowing that his friends would oppose this effort, he had on this occasion kept his intention secret, only revealing it to a single member of his family, and not allowing himself to be dissuaded, though earnestly entreated not to overtask his little strength. It appeared afterwards that he had an idea, amounting to a conviction, that this would be his last message to the people whom he had for so long a time faithfully borne in his heart before God, and he could not lose the opportunity of speaking to them once again, knowing how powerful, through God's grace, the words of a dying man are often found to be. Accordingly, he addressed his people from the Saviour's last request, "Do this in remembrance of me", speaking with the power and energy of health, but with the pathetic earnestness of one whose voice would soon be hushed; and especially, most earnestly and lovingly, he called on the young to lose no time before attending to their Lord's call. The sermon over, he was driven back to Shanty Bay, and from this time his strength steadily declined, though he hoped, almost to the last, to be permitted to speak once more in his Master's name.

His public work, however, was now done, and it only remained that he should so meet the last enemy as to illustrate the sustaining power of God's grace, to the affectionate circle of friends and relations who had access to him in his home.

The first violent attack of hæmorrhage—writes a member of his family—that hastened his end, occurred on August 8th, as he was feeling unusually well, and preparing to take part in the Church Service at Shanty Bay. The prostration which ensued lasted a fortnight. When able to leave his bed, his days were chiefly spent in an easy chair on the verandah.

Through the cool, mellow autumn days, his gentle spirit was in perfect harmony with the peaceful country life, and deeply he loved God in the loveliness of his works. The tender, quiet beauty of the landscape, as seen from the rustic Parsonage, was a never failing pleasure. The brightness of the sunshine found corresponding rays in his own heart. When his strength was very low, and a few steps wearied him, he still sought his accustomed place to breathe and enjoy God's sweet air, a gentle, resigned expression on his face, an expression even of pleasure, as his eye rested upon some fresh loveliness in the sky, and ever varying water. His affectionate heart, too, found much solace during the long afternoons in having his beloved ones about him, and genuine joy beamed on his fine expressive face, as he welcomed the arrival of those of his relatives who, from other ties, could not always have the happiness of being near him. In thankful patience he waited for many successive days and weeks, until God should call him to that place where all is perfect, where his eyes should behold the King in his beauty.

"His character, always childlike in its freshness," writes another member of his family, "the warmth of his affections, his impulsiveness, his sanguine temperament, and above all, his humility, became more and more saint-like as he neared the border of the promised land. He bore with the sweetest patience his weakness, and at times his great suffering. Remarkably unselfish, he ever thought more of others than of himself. Long after he was unable to taste more than one morsel, he sat at his table, well pleased to see others partaking with appetite of what he could not put to his lips. If those about him saw his face shadowed by pain, he hastened to assure them it was nothing, and at once put on a bright expression. So after attacks of painful weakness, his chief wish was to allay the anxiety depicted in the faces of those around him, and the first moment he could articulate he would faintly utter, 'I feel better now.' He became truly, almost perfected for heaven; Divine Grace shone so brightly in all his words and thoughts. One trait was, in his last days, remarkably developed. With extreme self-diffidence he listened with increased respect to the suggestions of those about him; not hesitating even to submit himself to the guidance of his children. Gratitude, also, was another striking characteristic of him at this season. Very appreciative of any kindness from his fellow men, he was never tired of recounting God's mercies and blessings. He thanked his Father for every thing, never murmuring at any part of his dealings, and coupling every wish for prolonged life, for strength in weakness, for alleviation from pains, with the pious ejaculation, 'If it be God's will.'"

A few weeks before his death, he said to one of his children, "If it was the Lord's will to spare me a little longer to my family, I should be thankful; but *He knows best!* He knows best!" He often said, "I am almost too happy; I wonder why the Lord makes me so happy." One thought seemed to give him unceasing pleasure; the realization of his being clothed in Christ's righteousness. Many times would he lay down his book, exclaiming, "It is a wonderful thought!"

The second attack of hæmorrhage returned at the end of September. The last week he was unable to leave his bed. A friend who saw him a few days before his death, was struck with his look of "heavenly contentment and peace." When he grew too weak even to hear one speaking, his heart and soul were still sustained by the one theme. On his last Sunday he said, "I feel too weak to talk or hear any thing. It does not seem like Sunday: but you can all pray for me."

To the last he was very grateful for the kind enquiries of his people, as also for the delicate, thoughtful attentions shewn by so many of them. His anxiety for the welfare of souls outweighing and outlasting all interest in purely worldly happiness, was remarkably evinced by an incident occurring two days before his release. He had written to a friend, to whom he was much attached, on the all-important question of his soul's salvation. Each time letters were brought into the house, he would enquire for the reply he so eagerly looked for. At last it came, and with this letter, one from his tenderly loved absent daughter, whose letters always rejoiced him.

At this time he had become so painfully weak that he could scarcely bear the sound of a voice. He expressed no wish to hear his daughter's letter, but simply asked how it was with her, and being told that it bore affectionate messages to him, and that she was in good health, he gently said, "That is well." The other letter it was feared might excite him, and therefore its contents were only alluded to; but he begged so earnestly to hear it, that it was read to him. He listened with a look of happy thankfulness, which his feeble voice could not express, and seemed *quite satisfied*.

The last portion of Scripture read to him, was, by his own request, the 51st Psalm.

The scene at his death-bed was one not often witnessed, and most touching. All his children surrounded it save one. God saw fit that his servant should suffer much, but He sent peace and calm before the end. When the power of utterance was almost gone, one of his family, who desired to hear from his own lips a few assuring words, put the question, "Do you feel your Saviour near you now, in the dark valley?" The answer came in laboured, broken whispers, "Yes, dear! yes, dear!

I am a poor sinner, but Jesus died for me; the just for the unjust; to save to the uttermost. I do not feel, as I ought, my sinfulness and His righteousness. I want to feel more my need of Him." Then after a few words, which were lost, "He has poured his blessings upon me; surrounded by my darling wife, and darling children." No more could be heard; but soon after he murmured, "Pray!" and with those he loved kneeling around the bed, prayers being offered by each in turn, and sweet comforting promises of scripture repeated amid suppressed sobs and tears, his spirit passed away, so calmly, sweetly, gently, that none could say at what moment the angel had been there to bear it aloft.

It was two hours after midnight when he departed. All that night the waves had broken heavily and loudly on the shore. How often he had listened to their murmurs in sunny days of health, and been soothed by their lulling voices through weary nights of pain. The autumn wind, sweeping in through the open windows, sighed mournfully through the room which for so many years had been the gathering place of a happy circle. His Bible lay open at the last words on which his mortal eyes had rested. Looking at the still and peaceful face, it sounded like a voice from the unknown world, "Let all bitterness, and wrath, and anger, and clamour, and evil speaking, be put away from you, with all malice, and be ye kind one to another, tender-hearted, forgiving one another, even as God for Christ's sake hath forgiven you."

His beloved people paid every possible tribute of respect to his memory. Two days after his decease (October 7th) his mortal remains were followed to his last resting place, the family vault at Barrie, by an immense concourse. Ministers of all denominations were present in the procession; an evidence of the large and loving charity which he manifested to all who were called by the name of Christ. It is remarkable that he was borne away from the home which had known him so long, on the twenty-seventh anniversary of the day on which he first beheld it. That far-off day, serene, and glowing with sunny radiance, had ushered in the longest period of his life's work. Under such an unclouded sky was he carried to his rest. The loveliness of the outer world was in sad contrast to the darkened home, yet not discordant; a type of the brightness of the land beyond the river, speaking of peace to the hearts of the mourners, and of comforting assurance that it was indeed well with him for whom they wept.

The mortuary chapel was hung with black, also the pulpit and the chancel rails of the church, where his voice had so long been heard; which mourning garb it continued to wear for its departed pastor during the eleven weeks which preceded Christmas.

The solemn funeral hymns of the succeeding Sunday awakened much painful emotion on the part of many, and the sombre dress of the congregation, showed how deep was their sense of the loss they had sustained.

There was no lack of feeling in the church at Barrie; but it was at Shanty Bay, more especially, that the blank left by the dear departed minister seemed most fully realized. This was only natural, since it was at the latter place that Mr. Ardagh had lived; and the people there being few in number had lived together almost like one large family. Here, on the Sunday after the funeral, the Rev. Mr. Morgan officiated, and when he gave out the hymns, which his emotion almost prevented him from doing, the people did not so much sing, as sob forth the sorrowful words; and, at other parts of the service, loud and continuous weeping was heard distinctly through the little sanctuary. So evidently and deeply was it felt that a kind friend, no less than a faithful pastor, was gone from them for ever.

At the meeting of Synod, in the same summer, Bishop Bethune, in lamenting the death of Mr. Ardagh, speaks of him as "a clergyman of singleness of purpose and blameless life, who for years devoted himself with energy and success to his work."

A number of resolutions were passed by various public bodies in his County, expressive of the loss sustained, and of sympathy with his family. They will be found in another place.

As a private Christian, Mr. Ardagh shone with peculiar brightness. "My impressions of his social character," writes one who knew him well and intimately for many years, "are all that is pleasing. His hospitality was unbounded; perhaps carried to a fault. Whoever went to The Parsonage was received with true Christian cordiality, and it was evidently a great pleasure to him to see not only friends but strangers seated at his table. His genial happy spirit, combined with the polish of the gentleman, and the sincerity of the Christian, made his guests ever feel at home. His manner was peculiarly cordial; indeed, he seemed to possess in a singular degree the power of drawing hearts towards him."

His love for literature was always to him an unfailing source of pleasure; the occupation of his few leisure hours in health, the solace and alleviation of days of weakness and suffering. All who knew him will remember the arm-chair in which he sat in the drawing-room of The Parsonage in winter, and on the verandah in summer; and the book or paper which was the invariable accompaniment of the short periods of recreation which diversified his busy life. The number and variety of the books which he read, will sufficiently explain what was obvious to those who conversed with him, his intimate acquaintance with the graver forms of modern thought. The solid periodical literature of the day, found in him a constant reader. The great Quarterlies, *Blackwood*, *Evangelical Christendom*, the organ of the "Alliance," and *The Record* newspaper, the exponent of Evangelical principles in England, were always to be found on his table.

Naturally of a sanguine temperament, he was ever looking on the bright side of things, and his faith and trust were very great. No matter what dark clouds loomed above him, his eye seemed directed beyond. He truly carried out our Saviour's lesson, to "take no thought for the morrow." When those near him would sometimes feel anxious, he would reply, "Why fret for what may never come? Let us leave the future in God's hands." In his case this trust was remarkably justified. In his younger days, with only a Curate's salary, and an increasing family, he was often left without a shilling. But invariably, through some source—often an unexpected one—sufficient came to cover present wants. This, the writer had from Mr. Ardagh's own lips; and in later days he loved to tell of God's goodness to him in this respect. His own means were never large, though his generous heart, and manner of acting, often led people to suppose the contrary; and never did he refuse to answer a call of want from any quarter, though it drew the last dollar from his purse. In later years (his children each inheriting from their mother a share of a legacy left her by her uncle, the late Col. Anderson,) he was enabled to carry out to a greater extent his desires in this respect.

Of a singularly forgiving spirit, the adverse criticism, or unkind remarks of others left no abiding trace of annoyance. Possessed of true charity, he bore ill-will to none, and was only too willing to forgive and forget.

He was very impulsive and quick to utter what was in his mind at the moment, with little of the worldly wisdom of reticence, and opinions hastily spoken may, on some occasions, have re-acted against him. But by any who knew him, they could not be resented; for there lay still below the large kindly heart, and any heat which he felt at the moment was soon forgotten.

"By those who knew him best," writes a member of his family, "he was loved the best." No higher tribute could be paid to true worth. He was peculiarly beloved and respected by his family, and never did a father better merit his children's love.

Among the many letters of sympathy received by his mourning family after his death was one written by a warm and stedfast friend of the family, who has for many years occupied a prominent position in Canada, and whose sterling worth and charms of person and manner are known far and wide. The following is an extract from her letter:—

"The news of your good and kind father's departure was a fresh reminder of the time that is getting every year further away from our own family party; the time, I mean, when two of my dear brothers, now gone, used to partake with us of the ever kind hospitality of Shanty Bay. And now so many of the old voices that used to sound so cheerfully then, are silent to us for ever! Ah! believe me, I am very, very sorry to think of the blank there will be among my kind friends, now that the loving and tender old father has been called to his rest—for myself, too, for I know that I have lost one whose interest was genuine and sincere, and whom I can ever remember as having been most kind to me and mine, when we came as strangers to the country. How many pleasant days spent at his house, your father's name must have brought to the memories of those who had been there, and who will remember his unaffected, simple hospitality, and the special power he seemed to possess of making every one at home who partook of it."

The following are extracts from other letters, the writers of which were clergymen:—

"Regards to all your circle, with a loving centre like you, that may well be of large, and yet well defined circumference."

Another, writing after his death, says : "Of all men living he held, uninterruptedly, the first place in my esteem, from the day we first knew each other, May 20th, 1824, till he entered into his rest. We were pleasant in our lives, and though in death separated, we shall be restored to each other in the bonds of everlasting love."

"My intimacy with your dear father was more during our college than our clerical life. Yet even then I saw in him, in embryo, the qualities which, matured by experience and sanctified by Divine Grace, made him what he was in after life, upright, just, and exemplary, in every respect."

"His missionary work was indeed a work of faith and labour of love, and one in which to persevere would demand the constant realizing of the Master's and Father's voice, 'Son, go work to-day in my vineyard.' One of the most striking features in Mr. Ardagh's character, was simplicity: to me, he ever seemed to be guileless. His indifference to money was almost a fault; he was ever ready to give equally with his means, and this generous disposition he retained to the last, if I may judge from his kind consideration of my little church, at a time when the demands of expiring nature would have occupied most minds, to the exclusion of all else..........However much those nearest and dearest to my late brother in Christ mourn his absence, they cannot but rejoice that he is where the strife is over, where the joy of their Lord is their strength. May the hope of a happy re-union stimulate us all to double our diligence in glorifying God and serving our day and generation."

An absent daughter wrote of him: "What principally remains in my mind is, the remembrance of his indulgent love for his children, his blindness towards their faults, his impartiality in judging the shortcomings of those who had no claim on his regard. Above all, his simple faith. I also remember how, when an opportunity occurred of engaging his offices of brotherly kindness or charity, he never paused to reflect how far he would be the loser, before holding out a loving, helping hand."

The following extracts from his letters, at different periods, may serve, in some measure, to illustrate his character :—

"February, 1849.—I have every confidence that you will not be led away by the fashionable follies of the time. I trust that after your sojourn in Toronto, you will be content with this lonely place. Remember your duty is here, and looking up to God, He will make any place agreeable. It is, at all events, sanctified by the glorious departure of your beloved mother."

"May, 1849: Off Waterford. — Only three weeks from Toronto, *without steam!* How thankful we ought to be for such a splendid passage. A great care, my dear child, rests upon your young shoulders; but I am free from anxiety. Do all you can to make the last days of the mother of our dear departed happy. Indeed, I love her for her own sake, as the world does not produce a more disinterested or unselfish, or more loving mother.

"You are all upon my heart, and I would be, if possible, a mother to you all, as well as a father. My happiness is intimately bound up with that of my dear children, for whom I never cease to thank God that they are what they are. I hope that your hearts, as well as voices, will be lifted up morning and evening for us and yourselves. We have prayers on board every day, and remember you all. Kiss all for me, not forgetting the little nephews, whom I hope to treat as my own children. May our Gracious God take you all into His protection, and shield you from every harm. Tell 'Aunt Bessie' I love her as a sister, and more than a sister."

"July, 1849.—As for dear M——, I shall never forget her deep attachment and devotion to her dying mother, to whom she was an unceasing nurse and companion. I can see her now, as I have often seen her, beside the sofa on which her languid frame was stretched. She is an affectionate, dear child. I love my dear boys also, and hope they will not disappoint my expectations.*.........I think that I have secured the services of an excellent clergyman. They are six in family. I think you must make room for them till I go out..........Invite whom you please, and as long as you like, to the house, and provide every thing comfortable."

In allusion to the loss of the steamship *Canadian*, in 1861, at which time two of his daughters and a son-in-law narrowly escaped death, he writes :—

" When I heard you were all safe, I attributed it to a mother's prayers offered up long since at a throne of grace. I firmly believe it. May God preserve you, and bring you back to a loving parent's heart."

---

* One of the blessings for which he constantly was grateful, was the grave character and filial devotion of his only surviving son.

"1867—A house full. Eighteen slept under our roof last night. E. is coming to honor your birthday; from a father's heart I wish you many happy ones after I have been mingled with the dust. I have a confidence that the union which exists on earth, shall be renewed in Heaven, and that we shall meet at God's right hand. I always believed that there will be a thorough recognition hereafter.........It is a consolation to have you all settled before I go hence and be no more seen, and my time is fast drawing to a close. I feel the shadows of evening closing around me, but I have every prospect of my sun setting without a cloud."

"March, 1868.—I have not been a single day well, and suffer from total loss of appetite. I think, sometimes, I am breaking up. I confess that I should wish to live a little longer, surrounded, as I am, with a dear, affectionate wife and children. I hope I shall be prepared when called for, trusting in the finished work of Jesus ....Although I have been so ill, I have not missed one Sunday in Church, but Mr. Checkley most kindly takes the entire service at Barrie, leaving me nothing but the sermon. With concentrated love, believe me, your affectionate father."

"Steamship *Nova Scotian*, June, 1868.—Give my most fond and affectionate love to my other dear children and their husbands, whose tender sympathy, since the beginning of my illness, has been such a solace to me. I cannot think of my children's affection for me without deep emotion. I have the delightful anticipation of meeting them all in Heaven, where sorrow shall for ever pass away.........

"It is an inexpressible comfort to me to have my dear wife with me, who is so devoted to my welfare in every way. For this I am indebted to the dear Judge. If the reflection of having made two people entirely happy, can be any recompense to him, he may enjoy it. I do feel now that the voyage was the only thing to restore me. God grant that it may continue after I leave the sea. I was perfectly astonished at myself, being able to have full service on board on Sunday, and again yesterday; two full services, one in the morning in the saloon, and another in the evening in the steerage, but went to bed dreadfully fatigued, and with the impression that I had acted imprudently. However, I found this morning, after a good sleep, that God was better than my fears, and did not allow me to suffer in His service. May God have you all in his holy keeping."

"August, 1868.—Your letter has just come to hand, with the expected intelligence of my dear brother's happy removal from all his sufferings here below. I have felt very thankful that he passed away so peacefully. I had before I left, the comforting assurance that his hopes of Eternity were placed on the Rock of Ages. May we all be found thus when called for. How happy to think that we are in the hands of a reconciled Father, who orders all our steps.........I feel that the lines have fallen to me in pleasant places. Oh! what reason I have to be thankful for all His goodness and mercy, which have followed me all the days of my life, and I have been so unworthy of the very least of His blessings. It is refreshing to hear that all things are going on well in the Parish. I hope to re-enter on my work with renewed energy, and work on to the end."

The next extract will show how, on the least amendment in his health, his thoughts were still fixed on his *work* and the prosperity of his mission :—

"October, 1868.—I have applied to the Colonial Church Society for a grant for £50 for Essa, and also asked them to place a few hundreds a year at our disposal there for similar purposes.

I am to meet the Board on Thursday, to advocate this request in person, and I have every hope of succeeding, as I found from a talk with the Secretary that they are in a pleasant mood to help us there, on account of the resolution passed at the Provincial Synod against Ritualism "

In a letter dated October, 1868, he says :—
" I cannot tell you how thankful I am to my, I trust, reconciled God, for His mercies to me, and for the prospect of a return to the bosom of my dear family, which I suppose I shall never leave again, except for a *better* home "

Mr. Ardagh took a deep interest in the many societies actively engaged in spreading the truths of the gospel. He was especially devoted to the welfare of the Bible Society, in which so many could meet on common ground; and it was his boast that he had been a member of it for forty years Amongst others that he assisted by his means and example; were the Foreign Missions Society, and that for the Promotion of Christianity among the Jews.

Such, in few words, were the life and character of him to whom these sheets are devoted. Who can read even the imperfect record without subscribing to the sentiment expressed in a letter from one of his daughters: "I wish there were a few more like him in my world! But it seems right, even to us, that the good should be taken away from trouble to their glorious inheritance! Who would wish to keep it from them?"

APPENDIX.

The children of the Rev. Arthur Ardagh were as follows:—

Samuel Brown, the subject of this memoir.

Thomas Reeves, who attained a high position in the Civil Service of the East India Company, and died in 1870.

Anne Brown, unmarried.

John Russell, already spoken of.

Marianne, married Col. Fishe R.A.

Arthur, who entered the medical profession, and practised in the North of Ireland. He died in 1861.

Rebecca, died unmarried.

Vernon, also in the profession of medicine. He went to India early in life.

Ellen, already spoken of.

Susan, who married Edward Long, Esq., M. D., of Dublin, and died in 1861.

William, who holds a situation in the General Post Office, in Dublin.

Two died in childhood.

The Rev. Arthur Ardagh himself died in May, 1846, and his wife in 1855. He was a most successful student, and the prizes taken by him during his University career were very numerous and valuable.

The surviving children of the Rev. S. B. Ardagh are :—

Elizabeth: married Henry O'Brien, Barrister-at-law.

Anna: married James Robert Gowan, Senior Judge of the Judicial District of Simcoe.

Martha Letitia: married William D. Ardagh, Barrister-at-law, M.P.P.

John Anderson Ardagh, now Junior Judge of the County of Simcoe: married Annie Maria, daughter of Edward A. Walker, Esq.

Naomi Emma: unmarried.

Marian Isabella: married Edward C. C. Foster, Capt. 12th Regiment.

James Anderson, his nephew and adopted son: married Amelia, daughter of John Power, Esq., of Glen Mills, County Cork.

Appendix. III

The following are the resolutions hereinbefore referred to as having been passed by various bodies, after the death of the Rev. S. B. Ardagh :—

By the Clergy of the County of Simcoe :—

"*Resolved*—That at this, their first meeting after the lamented death of the late Reverend Samuel Brown Ardagh, M.A., (for seven and twenty years Rector of the Parish of Barrie), the clergy of the county do hereby express their deep regret at his removal from amongst them; believing, nevertheless, that their present loss is his eternal gain.

"They would also tender to his bereaved widow and sorrowing family, their deepest sympathies in their affliction; trusting that He who inflicted the blow will also apply the balm.

By the Board of Grammar School Trustees, Barrie :—

"Moved by Rev. M. Fraser, seconded by Mr. William Boys, and

"*Resolved* — That the Board of Grammar School Trustees take this opportunity of expressing the great loss which they, as well as the cause of education in this county, have sustained in the lamented demise of their respected chairman, the Reverend S. B. Ardagh, M.A.

"His Christian conduct, his courteous manners, and his gentlemanly demeanour in presiding over this Board, greatly facilitated the transaction of business His earnestness and anxiety about the furtherance of superior education throughout the county, and his watchful care over the moral interests of the school, were of great service for many years in fostering and encouraging the educational interests of the town and surrounding country. While deeply deploring the loss of his services, this Board hope that they may not be deemed intrusive, if they respectfully and earnestly tender their sympathy to the family and widow of their departed friend."

By the Standing Committee on Education of the County Council of the County of Simcoe, and which, being submitted to the Council, was adopted unanimously :—

"In this connection your Committee desire to express the deep regret which they, and, as they believe, your Council feel, in the loss of *one* who, for more than a quarter of a century, so ably, earnestly, and assiduously, laboured in this county as a minister of the gospel, and for the advancement of education.

"They believe that in the death of Mr. Ardagh the community has sustained a most serious loss, and your Committee feel justified in expressing, on behalf of your Council, deep sympathy with the family of the deceased in their bereavement

"All of which is respectfully submitted.

"A. J. ALPORT, *Chairman*

"Committee Room,
    "Barrie, Oct. 20, 1869."

By the Board of Public Instruction for the Northern Circuit of the County of Simcoe :—

"*Resolved*—That this Board desire to express their most sincere regret at the death of one of their oldest and most respected members, the Reverend S. B. Ardagh, M.A. They also deem it due to his memory to state, that for several years, when education in the county stood at a low ebb, Mr. Ardagh endeavoured, with great energy and activity, to promote the educational interests of the district, and gave efficient aid in placing them in their present more favourable position.

"The Board at the same time take this opportunity of respectfully tendering their cordial sympathy to Mrs. Ardagh, and the family, under the severe trial to which they have been subjected."

Early in the year 1870, the congregation of Trinity Church, Barrie, erected in the chancel a handsome Tablet of white marble, bearing the following inscription :—

SACRED

TO THE MEMORY OF

SAMUEL BROWN ARDAGH, M.A.,

WHO FOR TWENTY-SEVEN YEARS WAS

RECTOR OF BARRIE.

A more cautious zeal and a more accommodating creed might have made his work easier, but he never placed either expediency or popularity in competition with truth and right. Constant and fearless, while youth and strength permitted, in the performance of the work his Saviour had given him to do, he yet acquiesced cheerfully in the wisdom which compelled him at length, through illness and pain, to cease working. 'Having done what he could,' when his strength was entirely spent, the worn-out laborer leaned on his Divine Master's arm, and passed into his rest.

He died October 5th, 1869;

Aged 66 years.

The inhabitants of this Parish have erected this tablet to his memory.

1870.

A MEMORIAL HOUSE, for the reception of Indigent Women, has recently been erected in the town of Barrie, and bears the following inscription :—

IN MEMORY OF

SAMUEL B. ARDAGH, A.M.,

RECTOR OF BARRIE FROM 1842 TO 1869,

AND MARTHA, HIS WIFE.

In honour of God, and grateful remembrance of Christian Parents, this House is erected by their Children.

1873.

A FEW of the sermons of the late Mr. Ardagh conclude this Memoir; given more for the sake of showing the character of those he was in the habit of addressing to his parishioners, than as examples of eloquence or polished diction.

To preach the gospel was his chief object; *justification by faith only,* his constant subject. His language, such that the most uneducated of his hearers could understand him: his doctrine, such that "the wayfaring man" could not misapprehend, inasmuch as it was founded solely on that Book, in reading which, "though a fool," he could "not err."

SERMONS.

"This do in remembrance of Me."—1 Cor. xi. 25; Luke xxii. 19.

From these words of our Lord, I intend to bring before you that great Christian institution which is to be celebrated this day. It is a subject on all accounts highly important and interesting, but one which seems to require a frequent and particular discussion, because of the ignorance, error, and superstition, with which it is so often accompanied. No institution in itself can be more plain and simple nor more obvious in its tendency and design, yet there is none which has been more generally perverted, misrepresented, and abused. What in itself is plain, has been involved in mystery; what is inviting, has been made forbidding; what is designed to soothe and pacify the conscience, has been employed to harass and alarm it; what is calculated to break men off from sin, has been used to make them easy under the practice of it. It is not, however, my intention to dwell upon these errors and misstatements, nor should I deem this the most profitable way of discussing the subject.

The best way of refuting error, is to establish the truth. What I shall endeavour then, in this discourse, is, in humble dependence on the Divine blessing and teaching, to state, in as plain and simple a manner as I can,

1st. The nature and design of the Sacrament of the Lord's Supper.

2nd. Our obligation to attend on this holy institution, and our sin in neglecting it.

3rd. The preparation necessary for a suitable partaking of it.

1st. With respect to the nature and design of the Sacrament of the Lord's Supper, I would begin with reminding you of the time, and mode, and circumstances of its institution. It was instituted by Christ himself in the same night in which He was betrayed, a few hours before He was crucified, immediately after having eaten the Passover, with His disciples, for the last time. Then it was stated that He took bread: 1 Cor. xi. 23. Such was the institution of this sacrament.

On reading this account of it, there is one reflection which forces itself strongly on our minds. Whatever might be the particular object of this institution, it was surely designed for the *benefit of those* for whose use it was prescribed. Can we suppose that our kind and gracious Redeemer, whose heart was ever full of love to His people, would appoint any ordinance for their use which would not be for their good? Would He especially, at such a time, when He was on the point of suffering the most cruel torments, and shedding His blood for them, would He then enjoin on them the observance of a ceremony which would not be highly useful and salutary to them? Would He then have said to them, "Do this," if the thing to be done had not been one, which He well knew it would be for their comfort and happiness to do? I dwell the longer on this point, because it is one which so directly meets the fears, and scruples, and apprehensions, of many persons who seem to regard this blessed institution with a degree of jealousy and suspicion, as if our merciful Saviour, in appointing this ordinance, had laid a trap and a snare by which they might be entangled and injured; as if, when He had invited them to eat of His bread, and drink of His wine, He had called them to do that which it would be safer and more prudent for them to leave undone. What an ungenerous sentiment is this! How unworthy of our Divine Redeemer! Does He deserve to be thus suspected by us? Is this a suitable return for all His tenderness and care, to tell Him when He calls us to His table, that He is only calling us to our *hurt*, and that it will be *better* for us to stay away? My brethren, have you ever been deterred from coming to the Sacrament by any apprehension of this kind? Let me beseech you to have more just and honourable thoughts of Him who loved you and gave Himself for you, instead of regarding with a groundless suspicion those symbols which He gives you of His body and blood. Oh! receive them as pledges of His love, to your great and endless comfort.

I now proceed to state: 2nd. Our obligation to attend on this holy institution, and our sin in neglecting it.

Let us consider in the first place by *whom* this ordinance was appointed; who it was that has said, "*Do this.*" It was Christ himself. It was He whom we profess to believe in, to belong to, and to obey; whom we acknowledge as our Saviour, whom we expect to meet as our Judge.

Let us consider, in the second place, that by absenting ourselves from the Lord's table, we seem in a manner to deny Him, and to intimate that we do not really belong to Him. Communion with Him in the ordinance of His own appointing, is a sign and badge of our attachment and relation to Him. By what mark is the Christian peculiarly distinguished, but by his profession of faith, and hope in Jesus Christ. At baptism he takes upon himself this profession, and he is signed with the sign of the cross, in token that he shall not hereafter be ashamed to confess the faith of Christ crucified. But if he regularly turn his back upon the Holy Communion, does it not seem as if he *were* ashamed to confess this faith? My brethren, when you have been going out of the church on a Sacrament Sunday, has your conscience never smote you with the thought that you were fleeing from your post, and deserting the colours under which you had engaged to fight manfully? Have you never heard a voice in your ear saying, "Wilt thou also go away?"

Let us consider, lastly, the loss which we are sustaining, and the injury which we are doing to our own souls, by not frequenting the Holy Communion. That it is an institution designed for the benefit of those who rightly partake of it, we cannot doubt, when we reflect on the power and character of Him who appointed it. As an act of faith and obedience, when performed as such, and accompanied with a grateful recollection of the mercies and promises of the gospel, it must have a very salutary and beneficial effect on all who are engaged in it. The very circumstances of having the pledges of our Saviour's love, and the emblems of His body and blood literally placed before our eyes, sensibly reminding us of His grace and mercy, of His death and sacrifice, and visibly assuring us of the truth and certainty of all that He hath done and suffered for our salvation, cannot but have a very strong tendency to increase our faith and confidence in Him, and to strengthen our resolutions of henceforth living more faithfully and closely to Him. I trust that many here can testify to the peace and consolation, and even joy, which they have thus felt while partaking of this heavenly feast, and can declare how deeply their hearts have been affected, and their souls strengthened and refreshed at this sacred ordinance. Besides, every exercise of faith is an act of communion with Christ. It is by faith that union with him first is formed; it is by the same faith that it is afterwards maintained, and while we ascend to Christ in faith, He descends to us by his Spirit, and thus we have fellowship with Him and with the Father.

If Christ delights to meet and make glad his people in His ordinances, in what ordinance may they so certainly hope that He will visit and refresh them, will impart to them spiritual blessings and make them glad with the light of His countenance, as in that ordinance which he has especially appointed them to use for the express purpose of remembering Him and the blessings which he has purchased for them, for testifying their faith in Him, and for solemnly renewing, as it were, their covenant with Him. But all these blessings we are voluntarily losing by absenting ourselves from this Holy Communion—neglecting the Lord's table, we are throwing away our own mercies. We are criminally depriving our own souls of that spiritual food which is provided for them, and consequently of spiritual health and growth, and strength, which cannot be but sensibly affected by such privation.

I come now to speak of the preparation necessary for a suitable partaking of the Lord's Supper; by preparation do I mean any particular mode or course of preparation which is to be performed previously to the act of communicating? Do I mean that formal, superstitious service, which consists in going through their week's preparation? No! The preparation of which I am speaking is the preparation of the heart; that state of heart which the true Christian habitually possesses, which does not consist in fancy and feelings, and which qualifies him at *any* time for a profitable partaking of the Lord's Supper. Are persons really humbled under a sense of their sins, of their sinful nature and sinful life? Do they sincerely desire to be freed from the practice and pollution of sin? Do they look to Jesus Christ as the only sacrifice for sin, by whose blood alone their sin can be washed away, and their soul cleansed? Do they entertain a devout and thankful remembrance of what He has done and suffered for them? If such be their desires, they have that preparation of heart with which they may partake, and ought to partake of the Holy Communion, whenever an opportunity may offer.

But there is one excuse, so very generally urged, that I am constrained to notice it. When invited to communicate persons justify a refusal, either openly or secretly, upon the grounds of their *unworthiness.* Now, my brethren, if the person who pleads this excuse, really pleads it under a deep feeling of genuine humility, if he is so truly sensible of the burden and defiling nature of his sins as to condemn himself on account of them, and with the publican to stand afar off, and cry for mercy—I can only say that of all persons in the world, such a one is most fitted to draw near with faith, and to take this Holy Sacrament to his comfort. If, however, those who plead their own unworthiness urge this plea on the supposition that they must bring with them to the table of the Lord some merit or goodness of their own, something belonging to themselves, which will make them worthy guests at His table, I must tell such plainly that they know not the first principles of Christianity. No man ever can have any merit, goodness, or worthiness of his own. If any one thinks that he has, or can have anything of this kind, he is vainly puffed up in his fleshly mind, and knoweth nothing as he ought to know. My brethren, trust only in the great and manifold mercies of the Lord; draw near to him with an humble spirit, and he will in no wise cast you out.

But those who use this plea of unworthiness have sometimes another meaning. Conscious that they are living in the allowed indulgence of some sinful practices, or some unchristian tempers, which they have at present no intention to discontinue and subdue, they know that they are not fit for communicating at the Lord's table. They have light enough to see that a course of sin is incompatible with receiving the Sacrament, but determined to continue in it, and therefore they plead that they are not fit, &c. And they plead aright, they are *not fit* for this sacred ordinance. And for what religious duty are they *fit?* Are they *fit* to join the service of the Church? Can they take part in its confessions, petitions, and thanksgivings? Are they fit to say the Lord's Prayer? Can they say to God, "Our Father"? No! the devil is their father, for by their own confession they are workers of iniquity, and consequently children of the devil. Oh, my brethren, if there should be any of you whose hearts at this moment tell you that this is your present state, think, I beseech you, how awful and perilous it is, acknowledging yourselves unfit to come to the blessed Saviour of sinners for pardon and life! Are you *fit* to die? You intend to repent hereafter, but you will not do it now. *No!* So you will go on in sin against light and knowledge, against conscience and conviction. Now, when invited to Christ, you refuse to come; Oh, beware, lest when you may desire to come, you find the door shut against you. "Now is the accepted time, now is the day of salvation." May the Lord, in His mercy, grant you repentance, to the acknowledging of the truth, that you may recover yourselves out of the snare of the devil, who are thus taken captive by him at his will.

"*For I have received of the Lord that which also I delivered unto you, that the Lord Jesus, the same night in which he was betrayed, took bread: and when he had given thanks he brake it and said, Take, eat; this is my body, which is broken for you this do in remembrance of me After the same manner also he took the cup, when he had supped, saying, This cup is the new testament in my blood: this do ye, as oft as ye drink it, in remembrance of me. For as often as ye eat this bread, and drink this cup, ye do shew the Lord's death till he come. Wherefore, whosoever shall eat this bread, and drink this cup of the Lord, unworthily, shall be guilty of the body and blood of the Lord. But let a man examine himself, and so let him eat of that bread, and drink of that cup. For he that eateth and drinketh unworthily, eateth and drinketh damnation to himself, not discerning the Lord's body. For this cause many are weak and sickly among you, and many sleep. For if we would judge ourselves, we should not be judged."*—1 Cor. xi., 23 to 31.

My intention this morning is to give (under the Divine blessing) a concise view of the nature and importance of the Lord's Supper. The expression contained in the 27th verse, and again in the 29th verse, gives to the consideration of the subject a *vast practical importance.* Laden, as we are by nature, with guilt, it concerns us to beware that we do not, in addition, become guilty of the body and blood of Christ Coming into this world, as we do, under sentence of condemnation, we may well dread to eat and drink an increased measure of it to our souls. We shall therefore endeavour to state the nature of that Sacrament, in which we are to-day invited to participate. The passage I have read to you contains the fullest account of its institution to be found in the Scriptures, and by taking it in connection with what is written in other places, we learn that there are five important purposes for which the ordinance was designed. It was designed as a memorial of Christ's death, as a representation of the benefits which believers derive from it, as a means whereby we become partakers of its benefits, as a pledge to assure us of still greater blessings in a future state; and lastly, it was designed as a token of the union which subsists among all God's people.

Firstly. I observe it was intended to serve as *a memorial of Christ's death.* This was undoubtedly the first and great end, "Do this in remembrance of me" That it was a memorial of his *death* and suffering, is quite plain from the 26th verse. Under the Jewish dispensation there was an ordinance which corresponded to this, and for which it was substituted. The passover was to the Jews, what the sacrament is to us When that wonderful deliverance had been vouchsafed to Israel by God's causing the destroying angel to pass over their houses, at the same time that he destroyed all the first-born of Egypt, he commanded a feast to be observed in memorial of this deliverance, which was scrupulously regarded by the Jews in after ages; and it appears that at every returning celebration of that ordinance, the reason of its institution was declared. It was instituted in order that the remembrance of God's mercy might be transmitted to the latest posterity. We have the following account of its institution, in Exodus xii. 24 to 27. Thus it is God's intention that the remembrance of that infinitely greater deliverance which Christ has wrought out for us, should be handed down through all ages, "till He comes again." And the ordinance as instituted by our Lord, is admirably calculated for this end. The breaking of the bread, represents the breaking of the body of Jesus on the cross. The pouring out of the wine, represents the spilling of His blood; that "blood which was shed for many, for the remission of sins." In the ordinance, Christ is evidently set forth crucified among us.

Secondly. The ordinance serves as *a representation of the benefits which believers are daily deriving from Christ's death.* The benefits are twofold. (1st.) Those which have been externally wrought out for us, such as the atonement which Christ made for our sins, removing guilt, procuring justifying righteousness, and securing for his people all those things which pertain to life and godliness; all this is included in the 25th verse: "This cup is the New Testament in my blood." There was a covenant between the Father and the Son. The Son engaged to make His soul an offering for sin, and the Father engaged that when this was effected, His Son should see His seed : Isaiah liii. 10, 12 verses." By the shedding of Christ's blood, this covenant was confirmed, and the cup was to be administered in remembrance of it, and was to be to all mankind a memorial and a sign, that on the Redeemer's part every thing was effected for the salvation of men; and that all who would embrace the covenant so ratified, should be saved. It represented that blood which confirmed the covenant, by virtue of which " all things pertaining to life and godliness" are secured to us. " This cup is the New Testament in my blood," is perhaps the fullest and most precious declaration connected with the whole subject to be met with in Scripture.

(2nd.) There are also benefits resulting from the death of Christ, which have been internally wrought in us; such is the implantation, maintenance, and improvement of spiritual life. These also are represented in the Lord's Supper; Christ represents himself therein as the preserver of that spiritual life, which He originally purchased for us on the cross, and infused into our souls by His Spirit at the time of our conversion. In the ordinance he spread a table for us, by the side of the altar on which He died, and there signified His intention of feeding and nourishing our souls to the day of redemption, as surely and really as His minister hands to us the bread and wine, those ordinary means of sustaining our temporal existence. This is a common mode of God's dealing. When He promises to bestow any great blessing, He confirms the promise by some outward sign: Genesis ix, 13, 17 verses. Again, when God would satisfy Moses that His people should not perish nor even be diminished by that thraldom in which they were in Egypt, He shewed him a bush, a dry bush, remaining whole and entire in the fire. It was a significant emblem of God's purpose, so Christ, for the same purpose, instituted and ordained holy sacraments in His church, to represent to His people the benefits He confers An in the *baptism*, the washing away of sins is represented, so in the Lord's Supper is represented the refreshment of our souls by the body and blood of Christ, as our bodies are by bread and wine. If it would not be straining the figure, we might observe a peculiar fitness in the elements of bread and wine to answer the purpose, not only because they are the most nourishing food, but because of the circumstances which render them so. To what process is it that bread and wine owe their grateful and nutritious qualities? is it not to their being *broken, bruised,* and *crushed* by the hands of men? And it is to the very same thing which gives to the body of Jesus the value, the 'saving efficacy which it now possesses. It was His being *bruised to death* by the hands of men, which made Him the bread of life? The best wheat, while it remains standing in the field, is not bread; and Jesus might have lived in Gallilee for ever; He might have taught in the temple for ever; He might have exacted obedience from the winds and waves for ever, and never been a SAVIOUR. Had He proceeded no further, He never could have been the *bread of life*. It was the cross, the wounds, the death of Jesus, that made of God's dear Son the *Saviour*. Not only does the ordinance represent the benefits we receive, but also *the mode in which we must become partakers of them*. Food will not nourish the body except it be eaten. Nor will Christ's death be available for our salvation, unless we feed on Him by faith, we must " eat the flesh :" John vi, 49th verse. We must feed on Him by faith, we must extract spiritual nourishment from Jesus by the habitual exercise of faith. It was not sufficient for the safety of the Israelites to kill the paschal lamb, it was to be eaten by those who were to be saved thereby.

Thirdly.. The ordinance of the Lord's Supper serves further, *as a means whereby we become partakers of the benefits of Christ's death.* We are not to consider the ordinance as a bare memorial of the death of Christ; nor are we to view it merely as a *sign* of the benefits we derive from Christ, but as *an instrument whereby those benefits are conveyed to us*, and in this respect, that definition of a sacrament given in our catechism is most just, " an outward and visible sign of an inward and spiritual grace given unto us, &c., and a means whereby we receive the same." It may appear extraordinary that such a simple means should be used by God for conveying grace to the souls of his people. But the means being simple, and apparently in no way connected with the end, is no reason for God's not using them. Is it asked what connection there can be between partaking of bread and wine, and receiving grace into the soul? We answer just as much as between the stroke of Aaron's rod and the dividing of the red sea Just as much as between Naaman's washing in Jordan, and the cleansing of His leprosy In all these instances God was pleased to make trifling instruments effect great things; and He takes precisely the same course in dispensing His grace through those ordinances which He himself has appointed. What is preaching in the estimation of the world, but foolishness? Yet it saves those who believe, and God delights to use "things that are not," in effecting His wonders.

The real efficacy of this ordinance to communicate grace to the soul when worthily received, is quite plain from the language used in 1 Cor. x, 16 verse· "The cup of blessing, which we bless, is it not the communion of the blood of Christ? The bread which we break, is it not the communion of the body of Christ?"

Again, if it conveys a curse to him who receives it unworthily, as we are informed in the strongest terms, that it does, asuredly it must communicate a blessing to others for this simple reason, that if the benefit to be obtained by the ordinance, when partaken of duly, be not proportionate with the evil, which is sustained under other circumstances, we had been better without it altogether, as we then should be liable to lose more than we could gain. But the benefit of the ordinance when worthily received, *is more than proportionate* to the loss where unworthily received. And we may apply, to this subject the language of the Apostle on another occasion, and say that, if by offence in the matter of this sacrament, judgment comes to condemnation, so by obedience in this matter abundance of grace and the gift of righteousness will flow into the soul by Jesus Christ. If we only recollect that Jesus "came into the world not to destroy but to save," we may be as fully assured that it diffuses " a savour of life" to the life of those who worthily receive it, as that it does the savour of death and condemnation to those who profane it.

Fourthly. The Lord's Supper is a *pledge to assure us of still greater blessings in a future state*. When first instituted, it was manifestly intended as a pledge of some future communion with His disciples: Math xxvi, 29 2, Luke xxii, 18. By this, He evidently intimated that a period would arrive when He would again hold communion with them in that blessed ordinance. That future communion is now partially realized. What St. Luke calls the " Kingdom of God," and St. Matthew, His " Father's Kingdom," is now partially come, and has been ever since the outpouring of the Holy Spirit on the day of Pentecost. Since that period Christ has been drinking it *new, i. c.*, under a new dispensation with His people, spiritually and really, though not corporeally. He has been among His people " supping with them, and they with Him."

But never will the Redeemer's promise be fully realized until it is completed in the eternal world. Then shall believers spiritually renew this feast: Luke xxii, 29, 30. Indeed, we read that Abraham, Isaac, and Jacob, are already seated at that table, and there Lazarus is described as leaning on Abraham's bosom, as the beloved disciple leaned on the bosom of Jesus at the Paschal feast. There shall all the redeemed of the Lord in due time be assembled, and then will the wonders of redemption occupy their minds as it does now when they surround the table of the Lord.

My brethren, will Christ himself again partake of it with us? Assuredly he will! "The Lamb which is in the midst of the throne shall feed us." Did he not break the bread and administer the cup to his disciples on earth, and will he not do as much, or more, for them in heaven? Mark that wonderful declaration in Luke xii., 37, "Blessed are those servants, whom the Lord when he cometh shall find watching: verily, I say unto you, that he shall gird himself, and make them to sit down to meat, and will come forth and serve them." Well may we say, "Blessed is he that shall eat bread in the Kingdom of God." My brethren, survey the glories which will then surround you on every side, and view the ordinance as a pledge of a better feast and purer joys in a more glorious kingdom; and though we are even now drinking it *new*, yet the time is approaching when the promise will be fulfilled in a far more complete and perfect manner. If I might use the illustration, I would say, regard it as a kind of title deed by which the heavenly inheritance is handed over to you, and your right to it secured; just as estates are handed over from one person to another, by a piece of parchment, signed and sealed by the original proprietor. So does our blessed Lord, our best benefactor, by the gift of the bread and wine, sensibly and visibly hand over to us a title to heaven. It was but a few drops of oil poured on David's head by Samuel, which transferred to him the whole kingdom of Israel; and in the same sense may we regard this ordinance as conferring future benefits on us. It was not the oil that gave to David a right to the kingdom of Israel, *that* was the gift of God, neither is it a participation in this ordinance which can, properly speaking, give a title to heaven, for that also is the very freest gift of God; but just as the anointing oil was a token and pledge that thenceforth the kingdom was his, so is this ordinance a token to the believer that heaven is his, and that all that Christ has to bestow in heaven, yea, even Christ himself, is, and shall be, his portion for ever.

Fifthly I observe in the last place that the Lord's Supper is a *token of the union which subsists between God's people*. A union exists between Christ and his people. They dwell in Christ, and Christ with them. But there is another union signified in the ordinance, namely, *that which exists among his followers:* 1 Cor. x 16, 17. It is a communion between the members themselves, as well as between the members and the head. We eat of the same loaf, and drink of the same cup, in token that we derive our spiritual life and sustenance from one common source, and are indeed members one of another. The first Christians, we know, partook of the ordinance with that object in view; and it appears to be placed very prominently in that light in Acts ii. 42, 46: "They continued stedfastly in the Apostles doctrine and *fellowship*, and in breaking of bread, and in prayers." "Continuing daily, with one accord in the temple, and breaking bread from house to house, did eat their meat with gladness, and singleness of heart."

"*Wilt thou be made whole?*"—John v., 6.

Suppose the question to be addressed to a man whose *body* is disabled, and that the person who proposes it is a skilful and experienced physician—could there be any doubt as to the answer? Would the patient slight the proposal? We may conceive certain circumstances under which he might do so. Perhaps he might not be aware that there was anything amiss with him. There are some complaints of such a flattering kind, that whilst they are gradually preying on the constitution, the person who is their victim thinks himself in tolerable health. What then would be his reply to the question in my text? He would answer, "I am whole already—nothing, of consequence, is the matter with me—only a little discomfort now and then; but I have no need of medicine." Or, perhaps a man may be aware that he is ill—he may feel the necessity of taking something for the restoration of his health—but then he may be possessed with the notion that he can cure *himself*. He puts faith in some medicine of his own, or in something which is recommended to him by a neighbour, and "where is the necessity," he may think, "of the physician"? "I can manage my own case well enough without resorting to professional advice." We may anticipate *his* answer—"No, I can heal myself."

But suppose the man is both aware of his disease—apprized of its deadly nature—convinced that he cannot cure himself, and very anxious to be cured. What then would be his answer to the question, "Wilt thou be made whole"? There *could* be but one, "Oh! can you doubt it; only tell me the remedy, and let it be what it may, I am ready to make use of it."

The man to whom the question in my text was put, was the victim of a most distressing malady of thirty-eight years' continuance, during all which time he had lain a helpless cripple; hoping, but in vain, to avail himself of the waters of Bethesda for a cure. He did not think it necessary to tell the Lord that he was *willing*. He was rather anxious to explain why he had lain so long before that healing pool without plunging into its waters—why he had a means of remedy before him and had never yet applied it. Our Lord knew that he was more than *willing*. He spoke the word therefore, and accomplished the poor man's desire.

We have considered the question in my text in its literal sense as addressed to one whose *body* is diseased, and we found that it might receive several answers. Some might think themselves so well that they had no need to be made whole, others might think that they could make *themselves* whole without having recourse to the physician.

Now spiritualize the question. Consider it put with reference to the soul, as proposed by the Great Spiritual Physician to those who lie under the disease of sin, "Sinner, wilt thou be made whole? Wilt thou put thy soul into my hands, that I may heal and save thee?" Such *is*, in fact, the tender, gracious question which Jesus puts to every sinner. And what answer does he receive to it? Just what we imagined it would be, when we spoke of a cure proposed for a bodily sickness.

Sin is a very flattering disease. There are some men who are sorely sick with it, yet without being aware—men that are living without God in the world—neither loving, nor seeking, nor caring for, nor thinking of Him. Yet deluded into the idea that all is well with them, having never looked into their own hearts, or searched in the Bible, and having maintained perhaps what the world calls an honest character, they are in their own estimation righteous men. So far from thinking that their souls are in any danger, they deem themselves to have a claim on the Almighty for the recompense of His reward. They talk confidently of their merits and good works, expect the praises of their fellow sinners as their rightful due, and never doubt for a moment that such as they shall go to heaven after death. With lives so respected, with hearts so good, with so many duties done, or sins avoided, who think they can fail of a reward hereafter? Sad, indeed, is their delusion! Alas! these self-complacent, self-admiring men, what are they? Wretched, ruined sinners—their goodness an outward show, their hearts full of evil and corruption. Whilst they are saying "We are rich, and increased in goods, and have need of nothing." He is saying,

"Ye are wretched, miserable, poor, blind, and naked." But the god of this world has blinded their minds. Their delusion is so pleasing that they will not be disturbed in it, and they go on quietly to their graves, saying, "Peace, peace, when there is no peace." They may, indeed, call themselves sinners, as a matter of course or custom, but sinners they do not really think themselves to be. What answer can they give to the question which Jesus puts, "Wilt thou be made whole?"

But these are not the only persons to turn a deaf ear to the proposal of my text. There are men who know and feel that they are sinners, and yet cannot relish the question "Wilt thou be made whole?" They are like those sick persons who think that they can cure themselves, and who will not for that reason resort to medical advice. Conscience tells them that they have sinned against the Lord, but pride tells them they have the power in themselves to make the Lord amends. Pride refers them to acts of charity and professions of repentance as sure and certain means of blotting out the guilt of sin. Never will proud sinners stoop to have salvation *given* them, whilst they think that they can *purchase* it. Are not "Abana and Pharpar better than all the waters of Israel, may I not wash in them and be clean?" Never, will the sinner wash in Jesus' blood for pardon, whilst he has anything of his own which he thinks will serve the purpose. He will rather "go about to establish his own righteousness."

Alas! then, how many are there on whom this kind proposal of my text is thrown utterly away. How many who give cause for the upbraiding question of Jeremiah "Woe unto thee—wilt thou not be made clean?" Jesus offers himself as their physician. He stretches forth His hands, but they, although ready to perish in their sins, will rather perish than resort to Him.

But is this the case with all? Is the Great Physician without patients? No, for there are some whose sentiments and feelings are widely different from those we have described. Such a man has been taught to see that the law of God is spiritual, but that he is carnal, sold under sin. He looks with horror on the life which he has lived, of vanity and worldliness, and alienation from his God, comparing himself with the holy rule of Scripture, he finds that all which he had done has been polluted, that unworthy motives have tarnished all his fairest actions, that "the whole head is sick, and the whole heart faint."

He is convinced, too, of his utter inability to heal himself. In vain has he used many medicines of his own, for he has not been cured. His vows and resolutions of amendment have been all to no effect; and as for his self-righteous efforts to atone for his past guilt, they have ended in bitter disappointment. They have not restored peace to his troubled mind and alarmed conscience. Every fresh attempt to satisfy the wrath of God has convinced him of his utter inability to do so. Every day's examination of his heart serves resistlessly to prove to him that if he be saved at all, he must be saved by grace, by a free and unconditional salvation.

Yet it is not from the *guilt* of sin only that he longs to be set free. He desires to have its *power* also broken and destroyed. "O wretched man that I am, who shall deliver me from the body of this death?" Glad would he be to tear out of his bosom this filthy and defiling inmate, to gain the victory over his corruptions, and to give the Lord that room which has been occupied by Satan. "Tell me," says he, "if there be any means within my reach, whereby I may be delivered from the bondage of corruption, and admitted to the glorious liberty of the children of God?"

To such a man as this, how refreshing are the words, "Wilt thou be made whole?" How differently do they sound in *his* ears and in those of other men! To the proud and the self-righteous, they are uncalled-for and offensive—to *him*, they are the savour of life unto life."

"Wilt thou be made whole?" is, in a spiritual sense, Wilt thou have salvation? And oh, how welcome is salvation to a soul that feels itself undone and lost! How joyful when that soul has brooded long over its guilt and wretchedness, and has seen its case deplorable and desperate, to hear that there is *hope*, that there is pardon even for its worst transgressions; that God's redeeming love has planned, performed, completed, an atonement; that "He hath so loved the world, as to give His only begotten Son, that whosoever believeth in Him should not perish, but have everlasting life"; that this is a "faithful saying and worthy of all acceptation that Christ Jesus came into the world to save sinners."

But the question, "Wilt thou be made whole?" implies also this further truth, a truth so comfortable to the self-despairing penitent, that salvation is the work of God alone. "Wilt thou be *made*"—a quiet, humble, and submissive patient in the hand of Jesus, not adopting any self-invented remedies, but committing all the cure to Him, making Him thy sole physician?

Such is the proposal of the gospel. How distasteful to the sinner, who fancies that he has the power of himself to help himself; but how unspeakably refreshing to him, who knows by experience his entire corruption, his miserable helplessness, to be told "You must contribute something of your own towards the work, you must complete the cure yourself, when Jesus has begun it." This, to a man who is willing to be cured, but who has a humbling sense of his own impotency, would be to make salvation void, and to place it out of his reach. But when he is assured that salvation is, from beginning to end, the work of Jesus, offered fully and freely to him who is willing to receive it—this is good news indeed, "Glad tidings of great joy." This is bringing near salvation, laying it in the sinner's way, placing it in the sinner's hand.

The poor cripple at Bethesda would have been told in vain to cure *himself*, but when it was simply, "Wilt thou be made whole?" the man felt that nothing more was looked for from him than his very helplessness could undertake, for willing he was, and willingness was all that was asked of him.

Viewing, however, this enquiry as partly in reference to the soul, it may be considered as implying much more than the pardon of past sin, when Jesus asks the sinner, "Wilt thou be made whole?" it not only means "Wilt thou be forgiven past iniquity?" but, "Wilt thou have thy heart sanctified, its thoughts and affections cleansed, the love of sin destroyed in it, the love of God established? Wilt thou be made a temple of the Holy Ghost, that He may dwell within thee, and regulate thy life and conduct?" To this the awakened penitent returns a glad reply, "Willing, Lord, most willing, am I that Thou shouldst rule and reign within me, and enable me to overcome this body of sin and death. Thanks be to God who giveth me the victory through Jesus Christ our Lord."

We have been considering what might be the sentiments of others in reference to the proposal in my text; but now, brethren, let us bring the question home—What answer are we ready to give to it? "Wilt thou be made whole?" says Jesus, at the present moment, to every sinner in this Church.

There are some of you, I fear, who care not to answer it at all, or rather by your conduct you are giving Christ a flat refusal, saying, "I will go on frowardly in the way of my own heart." But let me beseech you, brethren, to consider this great question once more. Let me call for a few moments, your solemn, serious attention to it. See how your case stands. You are in the Lord's sight just what you have confessed this day, sinners, "who have no health in you"; as such, the law of God declares your condemnation, the Lord Himself tells you in His word what you are to look for at His hands "Indignation and wrath, tribulation and anguish upon every soul of man that doeth evil." But He tells you at the same time what He has been doing for your souls. He tells you of His agony and bloody sweat upon the cross, informing you that they were all suffered for your sakes; that His love for you persuaded Him to undergo them; that they are the ransom for your souls, and that by *His* stripes *you* may be healed. He asks you then if you will accept of His good offices, whether you will come to Him for healing. He assures you there is no other way, that "No man cometh unto the Father but by Him." But that if you believe in Him you shall not perish, you shall pass from death unto life. All that he asks on your part is willingness to be redeemed—all that he requires you to bring is a humble, contrite spirit. "Wilt thou then be made whole?" Oh let not this most gracious question meet one more denial! Go, humble yourselves before the Saviour of lost sinners, and may that Saviour give you grace to say to Him, "I am willing. Jesus, thou Son of David, have mercy upon me."

There are those, I trust, among my hearers who feel thus minded at the present moment, thoroughly convinced of sin, deeply humbled under a sense of their own helplessness, anxious to place themselves in the healing hands of Jesus, yet you hesitate perhaps upon the point whether Jesus will receive you. Oh fear not this! dismiss every such apprehension from your minds—look at my text, and review it as a particular invitation to yourself. It was actually, indeed, addressed to another individual; but it is the style in which the Saviour speaks to every poor sinner. Couple it with other passages of His word, with "Whosoever will, let him take the water of life freely," and you need not hesitate to think that Jesus calls you in this passage to be healed by Him. Arise then, "be of good cheer, behold He calleth thee." Come with humble confidence to the throne of grace; and assuredly, as He restored health of body to the cripple of Bethesda, He will restore soul's health to you.

"*Behold, He prayeth.*"—Acts ix., 11.

This is God's account of a newly converted sinner. It is the way in which Our Lord Jesus Christ describes to His servant Ananias, the change which had taken place in the persecutor Saul. How short, and yet how significant and comprehensive. Let us consider what are the inferences to be drawn from them. And may the Lord bless and sanctify our meditations.

One inference they suggest to us is this, that a sinner's praying is a strange occurrence—"Behold, he prayeth." Behold is a word of wonder, and men use it when something strange and remarkable has taken place. It expresses commonly the emotion of a person who sees what is a very unusual sight. And what was the remarkable occurrence here? A sinner humbled in the dust —A sinner pouring out his heart in prayer. "Behold, he prayeth," says the Lord, as if He were Himself astonished at the circumstance. Brethren, how sad a tale it tells for human nature! Man calling upon God is a wonder: it leads the Lord to say, "Behold"! And why? Because the carnal mind is enmity with God. Prayer is a strange language to it, unsuited to its pride, offensive to its lusts, a burden more than it can bear. The natural man can use entreaty with his neighbours, he can ask, and seek, and knock at the door of a fellow creature; but to come with his wants and his entreaties to the throne of grace, to be a petitioner for mercy at the door of heaven, this he cannot be, he will sooner do without the Lord's blessings all his life, than go and pray for them. Ignorance always keeps him from the throne of Grace He knows not what he is to pray for. He is wholly ignorant of his own spiritual wants, and of what God has to give him. He may be aware, indeed, that to pray is an incumbent duty, that every man ought to open and close the day with it; but as he feels no sense of want, it is irksome to him to wait thus upon the Lord. Hence it is a wonder when the prayerless sinner first begins to pray. "Behold, he prayeth," he that never knew the meaning of a prayer—that worldly, godless man! Surely some strange revolution must have taken place within him ere he would thus of his own accord, and with all the powers of his soul, have called upon his God Nothing but converting grace— the all-subduing power of the Spirit could have wrought this mighty change.

Another lesson which my text teaches us is this, that real prayer is quite another thing from that which generally goes under that name. Brethren, you might suppose from the Lord's exclamation at the prayer of Saul, that he had never said a prayer before; that then was the very first time he bowed the knee, or offered up the language of devotion. But think what this Apostle was before the day of his conversion— a Pharisee, and the son of a Pharisee—a man of the strictest sect among the Jews: a sect who, however hypocritical, valued themselves upon

their long and frequent prayers. It could be no
new thing to him that he knelt upon his knees
at the time to which my text relates. Saul had,
many a time, prayed before he took that famous
journey to Damascus. And why then did the
Lord so remark upon the prayer which he offered
at that journey's end? "Behold, he prayeth!"
Just as if he had never prayed before! Brethren,
you will, many of you, anticipate the answer: you
will say, it was because the prayer he uttered at
Damascus was the first spiritual prayer which
had ever passed out of his lips. You are right.
Saul had often prayed as the Pharisees did, but
never till the hour of his conversion did he pray
as an awakened sinner. Instead of the proud
and formal carlessness of his unenlightened days,
he came in the brokenness of his heart, out of
the abundance of his complaint and grief, before
his God. He came, not to tell God his merits,
but to supplicate His mercies. He came, not to
perform an irksome task, but to relieve a troubled
mind. He came in earnest!—convinced of sin—
humbled to the dust—deeply anxious for the
salvation of his soul, and seeking it through the
merits of the Saviour whom he had hitherto
rejected. Now, mark this, brethren! it cannot
be too deeply impressed upon our minds: God
never heard Saul's prayer until he prayed in
spirit and in truth. All his Pharisee prayers,
however long, loud, frequent, went for nothing;
but directly his heart prayed, my text was
uttered—"Behold, he prayeth!" There are two
different ways of coming before God! Most

men only *say* their prayers. It is a *bodily* not a *spiritual* exercise—the knee and lip only are employed in it, God does not call *this* a prayer. He does not say of such a man, "Behold, he prayeth!" but "Behold, he trifleth! he mocketh Me! he deceiveth his own soul!" And this, however warm the language, however spiritual and fluent the petitions. But when the sinner, whose heart aches under a sense of guilt, brings his sad case before his God, anxious to obtain a hearing, trusting for mercy and for pardon, and seeking that pardoning mercy through a Saviour's blood; this is *prayer*, and what the Lord acknowleges as prayer.

The language may be rude and broken—the lips may be unable to express what the heart feels—but still it is prayer. The heart-searching God calls it prayer

But look again at my text. Does it not teach us something further? Yes, that God notices and gives an attentive ear to prayer such as I have described. What is the spectacle on earth, above all others, which His all-seeing eye is pleased to dwell upon? A praying sinner. And what the sound by which His ear is most engaged? "The sighing of a contrite heart, and the desire of such as be sorrowful." Let us call to mind some other instances of the Lord's attention to the sinner's prayer Look at the case of Cornelius. That poor soldier on his knees gained as much notice from the Lord as he would have gained from him had he been the conqueror of the world. "Cornelius, thy prayers and thine alms are come up for a memorial before God" Yes, sincere and fervent prayer, let it come from whom it may, is to the Lord's eye the chief of all events which happen on this earth. The poor, humble cottager crying to him for pardon, is an object more important in His sight, than events which agitate a kingdom and fill the world with wonder.

Come to Him, sinner,' with the sacrifice of a contrite spirit, in the all-prevailing name of Jesus, and you may be sure that the Lord of heaven and earth has his fixed attention drawn to you. His eyes are over you. His ears are open to your prayers.

I must call your attention again to my text. These are the words not only of a God who hears prayer, but of one who answers speedily. "Behold, he prayeth!" And what may we suppose, brethren, to have been the subject of that awakened sinner's prayer? We cannot doubt. He prayed to be led into the path of pardon and salvation, to be told what the Lord would have him do. Well, while he is in the very act of *offering* his prayer, the Lord is in the very act of *granting* it. While Saul is still upon his knees, begging light and direction from above, the Lord is answering his prayer by sending Ananias to direct and comfort him. And here then is one memorable instance of the fulfilment of that precious promise: "And it shall come to pass that before they call I will answer, and while they are yet speaking I will hear." Let any sinner here seek grace and guidance as Saul did on the day of his conversion, and behold, God's answer to that prayer is at the door! The Lord is waiting to be gracious. "Ask, and ye shall have."

But again, brethren, learn another lesson from my text. It is the mark of a real Christian to feel a tender interest in the conversion of a soul to God. Yes, and in the earliest symptoms of that blessed change. It was to Ananias, a faithful servant and disciple, that the Lord announced the tidings in my text, "Behold, he prayeth." And what does this imply, but that Ananias would rejoice in the intelligence, that he would share in his Lord's joy at the conversion of so great a sinner? "Behold, he prayeth!" As much as to intimate, "here is news that will delight your ears, in which you will feel a lively interest and satisfaction. There is a sinner praying, a fresh soul is being added to my flock." Yes, if a man's own heart is right with God, there will be no happier news for him than to hear that other hearts have been touched and softened. To hear of some hardened sinner that, "Behold, he prayeth," prayeth in sincerity and truth, will be music to such a person's ears, words that will fill his heart with gladness, and his lips with praise. How glad was poor Barnabas when "he saw the grace of God" at Antioch! How did Paul rejoice over Onesimus; and John over the children of the elect lady. You, brethren, that profess godliness, have you this mark? Can you rejoice with your good Shepherd over a returning sheep? Can you enter into such a feeling as dictated the words of my text, "Behold, he prayeth?"

But it was not only to refresh the heart of

Ananias, that the Lord communicated to him these happy tidings. The intelligence "Behold, he prayeth!" was followed immediately by a call on Ananias to water what the Lord had planted "He prayeth," and therefore there is a call upon your charity, there is an opportunity, an occasion, a demand for your offices of Christian love. Learn then, Christian brethren, that as soon as any ungodly neighbour shows any symptoms of a softened heart, as soon as it can be said of him that "Behold, he prayeth!" you have duties to fulfil towards him, you must hold out to him the hand of fellowship. You must endeavour, as ability and opportunity are given you, to strengthen him in the Lord. It is your part to comfort and encourage him—to speak to him of Jesus—to recommend his case to God, and especially to see to it that you put no stumbling block, no occasion of falling in your weak brother's way.

I have endeavoured, brethren, to draw many profitable inferences from a very short text. And I would fain hope that there may be some amongst the unconverted part of my congregation to whom, under God's blessing, I may have spoken words in season. O! if you *could* be drawn to pray, if, in place of the poor formal lip language which you give to God at present, prayer did begin to flow out of your hearts, what a fund of consolation and encouragement might you draw out of our subject! O! sleepers awake, and call upon your God! make the case of Saul your pattern and encouragement. Humble yourselves this day. Seek the Lord whilst he may be found, call upon him whilst he is near, cry mightily for pardon and acceptance through a Saviour's blood. That gracious, precious Saviour, stands nigh at hand to catch your earliest words of unfeigned supplication. And when it can be testified of you "Behold, he prayeth!" that prayer shall gain a ready answer from the courts of heaven. You shall be what Saul was *then*, and in a little while you shall be what he is *now*.

How happy if there be any souls amongst you who are beginning to feel what it is to pray out of the heart, whose prayer is no longer a dry form, but is beginning now to be a real act of crying to the Lord! Dear brethren, the Lord no longer hides His eyes from you. He hears you *now*. Your prayers enter into His presence. He inclines His ears unto your calling. He is exclaiming over you, as over Saul, "Behold, he prayeth!" O! avail yourselves of this. Improve your privilege. Pour into the Lord's listening ear your wants and your desires. Plead for Saul's mercies. Pray that his Saviour may be yours; that you may learn as he did to glory in the cross of Jesus; "to count all things but dung that you may win Christ," and be found in Him; to be constrained by the power of His love to "live not unto yourselves, but unto Him who died for you!"

"Likewise, I say unto you, there is joy in the presence of the angels of God over one sinner that repenteth."—Luke xv. 10.

We know very little of the angels, but what little is revealed gives us a glorious idea of them. They are creatures made by the same God, but infinitely raised above us in dignity and excellence. Let us consider the fact stated here by Jesus Christ—a fact interesting and remarkable—worth considering and which will, I trust, under grace, affect us as it ought to do.

Let us consider (1) Who the man is who attracts the notice of the blessed angels. (2) What their feelings are who contemplate this man.

First, then, who is the man spoken of in my text? He may be a man of any nation, of any country; he may be high or low, rich or poor, a king upon the throne, or a beggar on the dung-hill. These are differences and distinctions which, in the eyes of holy angels, are as nothing. The thing they look upon, the thing which draws their notice to the man, is his spiritual condition—he is "a sinner that repenteth." A sinner, one who hath done what he ought not to have done, and hath left undone what he ought to have done, who hath no health in him, and hath gone astray like a sheep that is lost—a sinner— one who has lived in sin, loved it, gloried in it, pleaded for it, committed it perhaps in every variety of way, multiplied it, perhaps, as the hairs of his head—

a sinner—one who has spent years, it may be, in the prosecution of his sins, "without Christ, without God in the world," but now, through God's grace, a "sinner *that repenteth*." He is brought to a stand, he is come to himself, he is ashamed, yea, confounded for the sins which he has committed.

In whatever way this blessed change was brought about, in respect of outward means—whether through the word preached or read, whether through public ordinances or private admonitions—in one way or other the spirit of God has touched his heart, and he is now a penitent, his sins are a burden and a grief to him, and his Saviour is his refuge, he has returned to his Father in heaven, and is saying, "I have sinned against heaven and before Thee, and am no more worthy to be called Thy son." His heavenly Father has graciously run forth to meet him, hath embraced him with the arms of His mercy, hath clothed him with the garments of salvation, hath covered him with the robe of righteousness, hath shod him with the preparation of the gospel of peace, and hath said "This, my son was dead and is alive again, he was lost and is found." He is now, therefore, become a changed man, "turned from darkness to light, and from the power of Satan unto God." This is the "sinner that repenteth." His case is little noticed, probably, by those around him, and few see it with an eye of approval, most of them, perhaps, are ready to exclaim, "The man was better as he was!"

But now let us mark, by the help of our Lord's words in the text, how the *angels* are affected by a change like this! One might have thought, judging humanly upon the subject, "It is an event too small for angels to take notice of, they have higher objects to contemplate amidst the glories and splendors of that world; it is not to be supposed that they should look upon an act of penitence which is taking place on earth, or if they do, that they should feel any interest in what they see." But what says our Lord? He, who knows all that is done or said, or felt, in the heavenly courts He tells us, that at the repentance of a sinner here on earth, the whole angelic company are filled with joy, and mark His words, "over *one* sinner." One might have thought, that if an event of such a nature could attract the notice of angels, it could only be when it happened on a large scale, as at the day of Pentecost, when three thousand sinners were at once awakened to repentance. But no, says our Lord, let there be only *one* sinner that repenteth and it is just the same. And observe, also, he says nothing of the sinner's rank or importance here on earth. It is not only when a *royal* sinner, or a *noble* sinner repenteth, but *any* sinner, let his rank be what it may. If it be a pauper, if it be the poorest and meanest of mankind, yet when that sinner repenteth, "there is joy in the presence of the angels of God." They are at *all* times a rejoicing company, *always* happy and triumphant, but *then*, it seems their joys rise higher. It adds fresh relish to their happiness, it makes their joy more glorious and more rapturous than ever, when they see one "sinner that repenteth!"

And observe, again, it is not one only, or a few only of those blessed ones, who thus rejoice over the repentant sinner, our Lord speaks as if the joy were universal, as if the whole innumerable company of angels, who are "ten thousand times ten thousand," all joyed alike over one sinner's repentance. His language leads us to believe that there is not one single instance of a true conversion here on earth, but it sends a thrill of joy through all the heavenly courts—that, if there could be seen in the meanest dwelling a sinful man or woman, yea, or a sinful child, upon his knees, humbling himself for his iniquities and seeking mercy through a Saviour, then there is joy in heaven at the sight, then all those grand and noble beings, who live high in glory, are transported at beholding it, and rejoice over it as a glorious event. What shall we think when we hear this? What meditations and what inferences should it lead us to?

Surely we cannot help exclaiming, in the first place, what an amiable and lovely spirit must pervade these holy angels, that they should take so deep an interest in man! Man is not akin to them—he is not of the same mould or frame—there is no brotherhood or membership between their holy nature and our sinful one. How then is it that they feel for us so strongly, and rejoice over our good? For the very reason, I may say, that they *are* made so unlike us. Had they passions such as ours, they might grudge at our improvement, and grieve at every mercy that was shewn to us. Had they anything within their bosoms of our envy and malignity, they might be glad rather to see us hardened and condemned than penitent and pardoned, or were they selfish like ourselves, they would be wholly taken up with their own exalted happiness, and care nothing about other beings, dwelling in another world. But having no such passions in their bosoms, being full of heavenly love, the case is otherwise. They can look upon our world with something like the feelings of their Lord, and as He delights in the repentance of a sinner, so do they. He, indeed, so loved poor sinners as to die for them, and is so well pleased when they are penitent and contrite, as to forgive them their iniquities. The angels cannot go so far as this. They cannot save or pardon us, or intercede for us above, but they *can* and *do* partake of the Shepherd's joy, when he fetches home the straying sheep. They can and do, gather round Him, as it were, and rejoice that His sheep is found, which was lost.

But again, let us learn from our text, what an all-important thing is true repentance? Is it so, that when a man repents of his sins, there is joy in heaven? And why then, is there this joy? Because it is not until a sinner repents that he is in the way of pardon and acceptance. For an impenitent sinner, Christ is crucified in vain. He is yet in his sins, notwithstanding all that has been done for him. It is not till a man truly repents that the blood of Christ is available. Till then it is as a spring shut up, as a fountain sealed. The man may talk of himself as a partaker in Christ's mercies, but he, in fact, knows nothing of them. He is still in the far country, still in the broad road, still erring and straying like a lost sheep, still dead in trespasses and sins. But true and genuine repentance is the turning point. It is when the leper feels that he is vile, knows that he is lost, is sensible he cannot save *himself*, and is distressed at his wretched state, it is *then* that he comes to himself, and begins in truth to seek his Saviour. Then, therefore, and not before, do the angels joy over his case. It is not when they see him baptized into .Christ's name ; it is not when they see him tread God's courts, frequent God's ordinances, and offer up with formal heart the language of devotion, but it is when they see his hard heart softened, his haughty spirit humbled, his high imaginations brought down, and hear that prayer of penitence arising from his heart, "God be merciful to me, a sinner." And do they rejoice in the first turning of man's heart to the God of his salvation ? What, then, must they feel as he *advances* in his course, as he adds faith to his repentance, holiness to his faith, "growing up unto Him in all things, who is the Head even Christ." What must they feel when they see him finishing his course with joy, and when they are sent to carry his departing spirit into Abraham's bosom! What joy when they welcome him into their innumerable company, and greet him as their equal and companion in the glories of eternity. Surely it will be their highest joy of all, when they see him numbered with themselves, and when he sings in a higher strain than they, his obligations to the Lamb of God.

But, my brethren, this joy among the angels over a repentant sinner ought surely to suggest some questions—questions to propose to our own hearts and consciences. Let me suggest two important enquiries of this nature—the first of them is this. Have *you* and *I* occasioned joy to holy angels? Are *you* and *I* repentant sinners? The answer must not be too hastily returned. Repentance, in the Scripture acceptation of it, is not just what the world means by such a term. Repentance, in the *world's* idea, is little more then saying with the lips, "I am sorry for my sins," or adopting, like the Romanists, some outward acts of self-abasement; but the repentance of the gospel is a change in a man's heart, occasioned by a real sight and sense of his iniquities. A sinner is said in Scripture to repent, when he feels himself a worthless creature, and is convinced that all his works and ways have been guilty before God; and when, abhorring himself for his iniquities, and acknowledging himself to be worthy of damnation, he casts himself upon a Saviour's grace, for the entire salvation of his soul, from first to last. And this repentance, which implies a change of *heart*, effected by the Holy Spirit, is sure to issue in a change of *life*. The real penitent cannot live on in sin, for which he has now a heartfelt hatred and abhorrence;

but he manifests his real sorrow for the past by an earnest effort, under grace, to mortify the sins he has committed, and to live a new and holy life, for the time to come. Now, has such a good work taken place in you? Have you ever been grieved and wearied with the burden of your sins, and have you really thrown yourselves on Christ to be washed and sanctified? If not, then there has been no joy on your account in the presence of the angels, but rather joy among the evil spirits, that you have never sorrowed to repentance. But will you say, "There is no cause for any repenting? none, at least for such deep and humiliating feelings as have been just described?" Hold up then the mirror of God's word before your souls. Measure yourself by His commandments, by Christ's sermon on the mount, or any other portion of His word in which your duties are summed up, and see how your life looks by it. See, whether on a serious perusal, it does not force you to exclaim, " If these be my duties, then I have never done them, if these be the sins I was to shun, then I have been guilty of many of them all my life." But above all, judge of yourself by your treatment of your Saviour. See how you have neglected and forgotten Him, who shed His blood for your salvation, and then say whether your ill returns to such a Saviour, do not constitute a sufficient reason for the deepest self-abhorrence. If these considerations do not affect you, then pray earnestly for a penitent and contrite heart, remembering that except you repent, you must perish everlastingly. Oh! there is no time to lose! To-day, repentance is acceptable, and a Saviour's mercies are before you, tomorrow you may find yourselves within a world where repentance would be unavailing, where indeed it is *impossible*, where they despair but repent not

But there is another question which those persons ought to ask their hearts who profess to be Christian people. "There is joy" you see "in the presence of the angels of God over one sinner that repenteth." Now is there joy in *your* hearts when you witness such a sight as that? Do you rejoice to see a sinner turn to God? for we have a nearer interest in every penitent transgressor than those who have never repented. He is our neighbour and our brother, and we have been his fellow sinners, and have partaken of the same grace? surely *our* rejoicing should be great indeed over every fellow sinner that repenteth? But, not only so, if we be really those who have ourselves repented and found mercy we shall be anxious to promote the repentance of our fellow sinners, we shall pray for them that God may give them repentance, and we shall be glad to assist, as we are able, those societies which are sending forth preachers to benighted nations to call them to repentance and to believe the Gospel Have we such a spirit as this? Are we earnestly and actively engaged in doing all we can towards the conversion of our fellowmen? if not, let us take shame to ourselves for our supineness and want of feeling. Look at the days in which we live! days in which sin exceedingly abounds, but days in which more is doing towards bringing sinners to repentance than in any former days since the age of the Apostles—days in which Bibles are circulated as they never were before, preachers sent forth to all countries of the heathen, a blessing extensively outpoured upon their labours, and a call therefore, an urgent call, addressed to you by God to assist in bringing sinners to repentance, and filling Heaven with joy.

"*And he turned him unto his disciples, and said privately, Blessed are the eyes which see the things which ye see.*"—Luke x. 23.

The great end of the Christian religion is to restore men to a state of well-being. We are in a ruined condition by nature. Amidst the general flow of animal spirits, and the quick succession of earthly enjoyments, in a state of external prosperity, and when our favourite passions are gratified, it appears, indeed, as if all is well with us, but it only appears so. For still there is something in our nature which is not really satisfied with all this—there is a void within us which all these things can never fill, and which creates uneasiness, dissatisfaction, and unhappiness. This unhappiness of man is recognized by all the religions in the world. Some promise this happiness in the present life—others in eternity. Mahomedans are assured by the Koran of an abundance of sensual pleasures in a future paradise, provided they follow in this world the directions of their Prophet. In the Old Testament various promises were given of temporal blessings connected with obedience to the commandments of God. But in the New Testament there is a further and special blessing which was not enjoyed under the old.

Now, in what does this peculiar privilege consist? in other words, what is it which constitutes the highest happiness of a Christian? Were I to put this question to modern philosophising speculators, who know nothing and believe nothing concerning Christ, except what happens to fall in with their pre-conceived opinions, I should receive from them a variety of answers. Some would say, "The highest happiness a man can enjoy is from acting the part of the good Samaritan—he carries about with him the consciousness of having performed a genuine act of philanthropy, and he reaps the thanks of those whom he has succoured, such things will afford a happiness not to be described." Another would reply, "No such benevolence ought to be exercised in secret without expecting or anticipating any reward—this would give greater pleasure to the heart, and would be laying up a good store for eternity. A third would reply, "The greatest happiness consists in the faithful discharge of the duties of our, station, and a man who does these must be in a good state, though he has no remarkable works to boast of." A fourth decides in a more general way, asserting, "A good conscience is the greatest happiness — feeling that we have led a respectable life, have done no disgraceful action, not guilty of robbery or violence, how quietly we may fall asleep on our pillow—how peacefully on a death bed with a good conscience!" I might add many others. What think *you* of these views of happiness? I will tell you what I think of them. They are only an additional proof of the blindness and folly of the human heart, and of the truth of Christ's words, "I thank thee, O Father, Lord of heaven and earth, because thou hast hid these things from the wise and prudent, and hast revealed them unto babes."

Wherein then consists the peculiar blessedness of the New Testament dispensation? We answer it consists in what is expressed by our Saviour in the text, "Blessed are the eyes which see the things which ye see." This is the essential blessing of the New Testament—that the Saviour is beheld. I will enlarge on this subject: 1800 years ago, in Judea, the Son of God was to be seen with bodily eyes, and handled with bodily hands, for He walked as a real man among real men. It was thus that His disciples saw him, but not on account of this that He called them blessed, others thus saw Him—but derived no benefit from the sight. The Pharisees and a great multitude saw Him, but they saw Him with eyes of indifference or enmity; of eyes such as theirs Christ could not have said, "Blessed are the eyes which see the things which ye see."

What was it then which constituted the difference between the sight which the disciples had of Him, and the sight which others had of Him? We answer, the disciples looked upon the Saviour with spiritual as well as bodily eyes. His words, His works, His life, awakened spiritual feelings towards Him, through the revelation of the Father vouchsafed to them, so that they could not fail to regard Him with the most profound reverence and love. The disciples recognized Jesus as the Saviour, the Son of God, whilst others took Him for a prophet, an enthusiast, an enemy, or a demoniac.

My brethren! it is with spiritual eyes that we must still, at the present day, behold the Saviour, if we would be the children of light. You may think that if you had lived in his time, and had seen His person, witnessed His life and miracles, you would have been among His followers. But perhaps you might have been among His enemies, for you, too, might have been offended at His humble condition. Every age has its stumbling blocks, mere bodily sight is not sufficient to make us believers. The eyes of your mind must be opened, the Satanical darkness that is in them by reason of sin must be taken away, the Holy Ghost must reveal and glorify the Saviour in our hearts. It is this, and nothing less than this, that can make any one a true follower of Jesus, and this was as absolutely necessary at that time as it is at the present. We must see the Saviour after this spiritual manner, or we are none of His— Without this, however well we may be able to converse about His religion, we are no better than hypocrites, or at least we know nothing of the real blessedness of Christianity, for it consists in spiritually seeing Jesus. This is not the utterance of a heated imagination, I speak the words of truth and soberness, yet there is a great difficulty in making it plain to you. Have you observed that we all have within us a kind of image or notion of ourselves. The mind of every one is, consciously or unconsciously, occupied in regarding this inward image of himself. Now while we remain under the dominion of Satan the father of lies, this image of ourselves is beheld in the mirror of self-love, and we thus appear to ourselves much fairer, nobler, worthier than we really are. Outward and relative circumstances contribute in no small degee to the formation of that notion of ourselves. Are we rich? Then we are apt to indulge an imagination that we are persons of consequence, who have no occasion to care much what others think of us, or to give ourselves much trouble about others. Are we in some place of authority? then the imagination of ourselves will be mixed up with ideas of power and importance. Are we poor? then we generally indulge a secret imagination of ourselves as persons ill-treated and oppressed. There are very few quite independent of this influence on their outward circumstances. So much do men deceive themselves about their real character, when they are not formed into simplicity and godly sincerity, by yielding to the influence of the Holy Spirit of God.

But the principal thing which I now wish you clearly to understand is this, that just as we have within us a secret image of ourselves, which as long as we do not love the Saviour, accompanies us everywhere, and just as we see ourselves in the deceitful mirror of self-love, so must we get the Saviour before the eye of our mind by the mirror of *His word*, and in the power of the Holy Ghost, and this is the blessedness of the New Testament. But we have not only this image of ourselves within us, but others also. Every one has some besetting sin, and according to it there are found imaginations in which our minds find their chief gratification. A licentious man has unchaste imaginations, and fashions them according to his own impure desires; a covetous man has imaginations of possessions, gains, wealth, and the soul revels in these fields of vain pleasure as long as it has no experimental knowledge of Christ. Now, just as this sinful imagery forms itself within us, so must the image of Christ be formed, and act with life and power within us. Christ, must, as scripture says, be formed within us, and become the supreme object of our love, accompanying us wherever we go, and separate from whom, we can find no rest or enjoyment. Christ must come into the heart, and be present to the eye of the mind. His Spirit must reveal Him to our spirit, else we shall not love Him, and he who loves Him not, cannot be His true disciple.

Is it thus with us? Do we thus see Him? O let us give ourselves no rest, till the Spirit of God thus impresses Christ on our hearts, and inscribes His name there. Then we shall stand at the foot of the cross, behold His wounded body, and His precious blood shed to atone for our sins, and by such a sight our souls shall draw in grace and mercy. How shall we thus be drawn away from worldly things, to commune with our holy, smitten, tortured, dying Saviour and Mediator. In the strength of this sight of Jesus, we can overcome sin, break its power, triumph over *selfishness*, —that most deeply rooted plague of our hearts— by its means, the imagery of sin is forced out of the chambers of the heart, as Jesus gains the ascendancy—yea, the idol *self* appears deformed by the side of the image of Jesus, a new life, a new self, a new man, Jesus Christ, arises in the heart.

Behold! this is the blessedness of the New Testament, the whole economy of the Christian dispensation points at this, and every ordinance of the Christian Church has this one object in view, namely, to bring Christ into the heart, to make us see Him with the eyes of our understanding. At the Lord's Supper the crucified Saviour is exhibited to us with His body broken, and His blood poured out, in the meat and drink which is presented to us to partake of, and as for the ordinance of preaching the word of God, what is its main business? It is to set forth before our eyes Jesus Christ as crucified among us: it is to make us acquainted with Him who died for us and rose again, and to shew forth the witness of Him "Who hath called us out of darkness into His marvellous light." Jesus the Saviour is the centre of all religion, Him we must find, possess, and behold, with the eyes of our mind, otherwise *we cannot* behold, possess, find heaven or salvation, for *He is* salvation.

2. I have now briefly to set before you *how we may* attain this peculiar grace of the new covenant. An intelligent thinking person who has, however, no spiritual experience, hearing what I have said, will be ready to regard all about spiritually beholding the Saviour, as nothing better than an idle imagination, as a mere dreaming fancy of my own invention—as the effusions of an over-excited mind, as mere folly, or, as at the best, the

sayings of a well-meaning but useless enthusiast, or as well meant ideas and notions, which are however of no real use to the world. This is the judgment which unrenewed men form of spiritual things in general, and of this grace and blessedness in particular, a thing which they understand not, which they can no more discern, than a blind man, scarlet, from Oxford gray. Such a man, as Newton said, is trying to light his candle with the extinguisher on. But this does not perplex or surprise us. "The natural man receiveth not the things of the Spirit of God for they are foolishness unto him, neither can he know them, for they are spiritually discerned." But oh! that those who are so ready to attribute spiritual experience to mere fruits of imagination, would for once give themselves the trouble of trying whether they can attain to such experience by any stretch or power of imagination, surely they would soon find that they do not grow upon any soil of our own. A man may, by his imagination, find his way into whatever is of human origin and submitted to the senses, and walk abroad among the sublimest objects of human knowledge, but as to the Saviour and His plain matter of fact history, especially as to His deep humiliation and obedience unto death, even the death of the cross. As to making *Him* the dearest object of his imagination, this is what a man without grace *cannot* do —here there is a barrier in his way, which mere human effort or reason *cannot* remove. In a merely natural man, Christ can never be formed, the soul will never feed upon Him, for there is an opposing will, an hostility against Him and His cross, within us, and this hostility we cannot get rid of, by the power of fancy or of human reason. We cannot drive it away. We cannot charm it away. We cannot will it away. It has grown with our growth, and strengthened with our strength. It is a constituent part of our very nature—yes, our reason, our knowledge, our intellect, the ground of our heart and the imaginations of our thoughts are in gross darkness as to spiritual things until the Spirit of God shines upon us.

From what has been said, it is easy to perceive how we are to become possessed of the special grace and blessedness of the New Testament It must be given us from above. Christ must be revealed in us by the Holy Spirit, and we can do nothing in the matter except to pray for this distinguished grace, and amidst this inward supplication, meditate on the Holy Scriptures, which throughout testify of Jesus, if, perhaps, it may please the Lord, by means of His written word of inspiration, to pour light upon our souls. Be assured, my brethren, that the Saviour is ready to make our impoverished souls partake of every kind of blessedness, and to pour consolation into them. The love of that adorable Redeemer with which He, while on earth, so affectionately and promptly comforted the weary and heavy laden who resorted to Him—the love of Him whose own blood, whose own life, were not counted too dear to Him for the sake of making human souls blessed and happy—that same love will not delay in manifesting to a poor penitent son or daughter of Adam, all the riches of His mercy. But we too often stand in His way. We do not suffer His light to find its way to our hearts, sometimes through some secret wickedness harboured therein, and sometimes when we have good intentions in the main. Thus it is that men remain poor indeed in the midst of plenty, without Christ, without the enjoyment of His grace, unblessed and dark. To a soul that sincerely seeks Him, to a poor heart which has nothing, absolutely nothing, of its own righteousness any longer to look to, which has completely humbled itself under the condemnation of the law, and feels that it neither can nor would cover its own weakness any longer. To such an one Jesus reveals and manifests Himself, and this too at the very time and hour when the heart falls down deepest into this loneliness and humiliation.

Oh Thou great Shepherd of the once lost, but now found and recovered sheep, bring it to pass with us, with me, with these, that Thou mayest become our *one thing* needful, and our all, that Thy sufferings and death, Thy love even unto death, may be impressed upon our poor cold hearts, never to be obliterated. Oh! we have long enough forgotten Thee! We have long enough taken pleasure in that which is grovelling; but now, Thou Sun of righteousness, arise upon us with healing in Thy beams, and dispel the natural darkness from our eyes and our hearts!

Printed in the USA
CPSIA information can be obtained
at www.ICGtesting.com
LVHW021027070124
768340LV00005B/160